Anishnaabe World

A *Survival* Guide for Building Bridges
between Canada and First Nations

by
Roger Spielmann

illustrated by
Perry McLeod-Shabogesic and Tim Steven

Your Scrivener Press

Library and Archives Canada Cataloguing in Publication

Spielmann, Roger Willson, 1951-
    Anishnaabe world : a survival guide to building bridges between Canada and
First Nations / by Roger Spielmann ; illustrated by Perry McLeod-Shabogesic and
Tim Steven.

Includes bibliographical references.
ISBN 978-1-896350-37-0

    1. Ojibwa Indians—Canada. 2. Whites—Canada—Relations with Indians.
3. Whites—Canada—Relations with Indians—History. 4. Ojibwa Indians—
Canada—Government relations. 5. Indians of North America—Canada. 6. Indians
of North America—Canada—Government relations. 7. Canadian wit and humour
(English). I. Title.

E78.C2S663 2009   971.004'97333   C2009-904230-4

Book design: Laurence Steven; Cover design: Chris Evans and Tim Steven
Cover and interior illustrations: Perry McLeod-Shabogesic and Tim Steven
Author photo: Melissa Stringer

Your Scrivener Press, 465 Loach's Road, Sudbury, Ontario, Canada, P3E 2R2
info@yourscrivenerpress.com www.yourscrivenerpress.com

We acknowledge the support of the Canada Council for the Arts and the
Ontario Arts Council for our publishing program.

Canada Council   Conseil des Arts
for the Arts   du Canada

ONTARIO ARTS COUNCIL
CONSEIL DES ARTS DE L'ONTARIO

Table of Contents

Dedication

This book is dedicated to my three beautiful daughters:

Jennifer, Melissa, and Stephanie,

who taught me the meaning of unconditional love.

The book is also dedicated, of course, to all the Anishnaabe people

who have helped shape my earthwalk thus far.

You know who you are.

Preface
and
Acknowledgements

Anishnaabe World is a hopeful book. Despite the deep, long-standing, and seemingly intractable divides between the nation of Canada and the First Nations that live in this land *now called* Canada, I am increasingly hopeful that we will build bridges across these divides and shape a new social, political, and moral landscape in this country. While I'm a hopeful kind of guy to begin with (which surely helps), my sense of the genuine possibility for bridging the cultural chasms comes out of two life-shaping experiences I've had, and continue to have.

First, my family and I lived for 11 years in Pikogan, an Anishnaabe community in northwest Quebec. We simply *became* part of that community, learning its language and practicing its values. Yet we didn't forget our Canadian values; in effect we became bilingual and bicultural (wouldn't Pierre Trudeau be proud!). And the community members embraced us, while knowing we were different. When I left to take a university job in Sudbury, the Elders urged me to share their stories with Canadians, which I did in my earlier book on Ojibwe discourse, and which I'm doing here for a wider, more general audience.

Second, over the past twenty years I've been fortunate to have numerous Canadians sitting alongside First Nations students in my Native Studies courses. I've seen first hand the real interest Canadians have in learning about First Nations culture. And though there are exceptions to every rule, generally the Aboriginal students are accepting of the non-cultural members in their midst. There is, however, a significant impediment to the classroom conversation, an impediment that has led directly to this book. Having a class divided between students who grew up as Aboriginal people and students who, with rare exceptions, know very little about the history of relations between First Nations and the government of Canada can be a pedagogical challenge both for the teacher and the students. Which group should the prof address? As I thought it over I came to a realization. While my classroom in some sense *embodies* the broader divides in the country, I realized that many of these divisions were due to the lack of a shared understanding that could enable conversation to happen.

Preface

So, how could my colleagues and I make our classes engage *both* sets of students? I began thinking, "What if there was an easy-to-read, non-academic book available to bring the non-Native students up to speed about the *basic issues* at play in our country today with regard to Native/non-Native relations? And what if that book was still funny and informative enough to keep the interest of the Native students?" Thus, the earliest versions of *Anishnaabe World* were born, as class supplements. And they worked! The students—all of them—laughed and argued and learned.

And then I had another realization...maybe this would work for Canadian readers generally. Well...here it is. You'll be the judge. I expect some of you are going to love it and others may hate it, but my hope is that this wee book will help us learn a bit more of that hard lesson we're facing: how to co-exist peacefully in this wonderful land now known as *Canada*.

A few acknowledgements are in order. First to the University of Toronto Press, for permission to reprint passages from my earlier book—*"You're So Fat!": Exploring Ojibwe Discourse*—published in 1998. © University of Toronto Press, Inc. Reprinted with permission of the publisher.

My illustrators/collaborators—Perry McLeod-Shabogesic and Tim Steven—added a whole other dimension to this book. I am in awe, and thank them sincerely. I especially thank Perry for permission to reproduce © cartoons from his *Baloney &* *Bannock* series.

I want to thank Laurence Steven of Your Scrivener Press for his keen sense of humour and his (at times exasperating) quest for perfection.

Diane Beck provided excellent research assistance and I appreciate her efficiency, resourcefulness, and friendship.

The University of Sudbury provided much needed moral and financial support throughout the gestation of *Anishnaabe World*.

To all of you, *Gichii-miigwetch!*

All author royalties will be donated to the Native Students Association at Laurentian University.

Roger Spielmann
August, 2009

1

Getting Our Bearings

"Okay," you're most likely asking yourself, "so what exactly does *Anishnaabe* mean, and what kind of *survival guide* is this supposed to be, anyway?" Let's take these questions one at a time. First, if you're not sure what the term *Anishnaabe* means, or how to pronounce it, then you probably aren't one, which means you *are* in my primary audience. "Anishnaabe" (Aw-nish-**naa**-bay) is the most common term used for group self-identification among Aboriginal people who live around the Great Lakes—Ojibwe/Chippewa, Algonquin/Nipissing, Saulteaux/Missisauga, Odawa, Delaware, Potawatomi and Oji-cree—because of its unique, culture-specific meaning as "The First Peoples." One Algonquin Elder with whom I spoke offered some distinctive Anishnaabe humour with his explanation that the word could be broken down into two components: "aanishnaa" (roughly translated as "just for fun") and "naabe" (man)—loosely translated as "Playboy." The important thing to keep in mind, especially for non-Aboriginals, is that "Anishnaabe" is the term that people use to identify themselves, and that acknowledging and using the term is a show of respect for Anishnaabe people, wouldn't you agree?

"But," you might say, "there are a lot of terms referring to, ah, Anishnaabe people. Can't I say Aboriginal? Or Native? Or First Nations? Or maybe even…Indian?" I heard that hesitation over "Indian." You're not sure about that one are you? Well, I'll admit things are a bit fluid currently. As Drew Hayden Taylor says, "The Pow wows they are a changin'." Some Anishnaabe people think "Indian" is okay; others HATE it, and hate you if you use it. But like I said a moment ago, it's really a matter of respect, and taking your lead from what they prefer. And I mean, use your noggin! The preferred term isn't going to be "chief," or "savages," or any of those cheap shots, like when you meet an Asian person and he tells you his name is "Sungzhou" (or whatever) and you can't pronounce it so you say, "Well, I'll just call you Sam." Not much respect there, right? Think of it this way: much has been written over the years about what cultural linguists refer to as "in-group" language and "out-group" language. In many First Nations communities, for example, it's common to hear community members refer to each other as "Nish" or "Neechee" or "Redskin" or "Indian" (even for those who HATE the term when *you* use it). Such usages are for joking and teasing, but, most importantly, for expressing "in-group" solidarity. Like when I worked with African-American youth one summer in Dallas, Texas, the use of the term "nigger" was commonplace among them, as in: "Hey, he's one bad nigger" (a compliment!), or, "Hey, nigger, what is it?" But if a *white* person were to use the term "nigger," that person risked being seriously, well, killed. It's kind of the same with a lot of my Anishnaabe buddies and the terms non-Natives use when talking or writing about them. The point to remember is that every cultural group uses and responds to "in-group" language, which those outside the culture are not invited to use until they've become quite acculturated, meaning they've hung around long enough to be accepted. So, given the language flux we're in, you'd be best off sticking with Anishnaabe until such time as the in-group indicates you're part of the club. You'll know when that is.

A quick addendum to the above story: one of my most moving experiences when working with the black youth in Dallas that summer happened the day I was leaving: one of my best friends came up to me and paid me a wonderful compliment. The group had called me "Catfish" because I wore a moustache along with my ponytail, and he said to me, "Catfish, you *awmost* be a Niggah!" Definitely one of the coolest compliments I've ever received! Similarly, when I told my friends I was leaving the rez to take a job teaching at a university, one of my best friends said something quite similar. "Shognosh," he told me, "you *awmost* be an Indian!" Another stellar compliment, in my book.

Now, what was that second question? Oh yeah, "What kind of survival guide is this book?" It's a light-hearted and occasionally sharp-edged *cultural primer* for non-Anishnaabe, non-First Nations people who *live* in this country now called *Canada* but who still really don't know all that much about Aboriginal people. In short, it's mostly for Canadians, although I'm pretty sure my Anishnaabe buddies will get a kick out of it, too. Over the last generation a new and often perplexing vocabulary has entered the English language: Aboriginal, Native, First Nation, residential schools, treaty rights, self-governance, native sovereignty, land claims, restorative justice, healing circles, Truth and Reconciliation Commission, Native Spirituality, pow wows, sweat lodges, clan system, and so on. It joins a set of terms bequeathed to us from earlier generations: Indian, reservation, tribe, chief, Band Council, bows and arrows, tomahawk, "ugh," "how," *kemosabe* (he who hides his face). Hey, it *can* get confusing. Some of these terms are current and cool; others are politically incorrect, to put it mildly. Picking your way through the language can be a bit like negotiating a cultural and political minefield. You need a trustworthy guide. One who has actually traversed the territory and survived! Enter *moi*.

At first glance it may seem kind of strange for a non-Native dude to be collaborating with a couple of artists—one Anishnaabe and one Canadian—to write a book about Native ways of thinking and doing things, especially a book designed primarily for people of the non-Native variety. But for a survivor it's not that strange at all; in fact it's what we aspire to for all readers of this book: a level of cross-cultural awareness and sophistication that will allow this country *now called* Canada to really be our home and *Native* land! How am I a survivor? Well, though I did not grow up as an Aboriginal person in Canada, I did have the wonderful privilege of spending eleven years living in the Anishnaabe community of Pikogan in northwest Quebec—and surviving it! I've learned to speak an incredibly complex Aboriginal language—and survived it! I've earned a PhD in anthropology—and survived it! And I've taught Native Studies at the University of Sudbury for 20+ years—and survived it (at least up to this point...)! For what it's worth, and it means a heck of a lot to me, Chief Gordon Polson of the Algonquin First Nation says this book "...captures the essence of the author himself, and how one can be literally transformed by living with Anishnaabe people." And when none other than Chief Ovide Mercredi, former National Chief of the Assembly of First Nations, tells readers to "really listen to what Spielmann is saying," well, that's cred, bro! And I appreciate the source. So, you might as well buckle up for the ride!

There's a great deal of confusion, tension and misunderstanding between Anishnaabe people and non-Native Canadians in this country now known as Canada. Surely Oka and Ipperwash showed us that in the 90s, and the controversy over the Residential Schools Truth and Reconciliation Commission is showing us the same tension currently. And it doesn't look like it's going to get any better real soon. But we live in hope. I frequently get asked by non-Native people—students and others—what some of the basic cultural differences are between Anishnaabe people and Canadians and how those cultural differences reflect different ways of thinking and doing things and therefore can lead to cross-cultural misunderstandings and tension between indigenous (homeland) peoples and European-based peoples in Canada. And the fact that I am asked, and that I'm a survivor, gives me hope for the relationship between Anishnaabe people and Canadians. I believe that "understanding each other" is something we need to cultivate, together. I figure we're all in this whether we like it or not, so we might as well learn to make the best of it. And, hey, maybe we'll see that it's not so bad for each of us to get to know what the other is all about. I am convinced that a basic understanding of some of these cultural differences goes a long way towards establishing mutual respect and a sense of *different yet equal* between

Anishnaabe people and Canadians. It sure did for me. I bet it can for you.

So, *Anishnaabe World* is not just some white guy writing yet another book about "Indians;" it's a collaborative effort with an artist who grew up as an Aboriginal person in Canada— Perry McLeod-Shabogesic, of the Crane Clan, Nipissing First Nation, and an artist who grew up as a Canadian person in, well, Canada—Tim Steven. Anyway, when I get out of line, Perry's not too shy to give me a kick in the ass and say, "Hey, Shognosh (the common Anishnaabe term for "White Guy"), get back to Anishnaabe reality!" And when I get too confusing, Tim's not too shy to say, "huh?" Kind of a salt-and-pepper approach, but guaranteed to keep the book real in representing both the Anishnaabe perspective, and the perspective of non-Native Canadians who find themselves a bit confused about Anishnaabe people and concerns in Canada.

So let's start off with a few basic questions that kind of helped to guide us as we were putting this book together. Like, why is it that most Canadians we've talked with over the years were *outraged* by the system of Apartheid in South Africa but were (and still are) indifferent to the system of Apartheid which continues to exist in Canada? If you're wondering, "What the hell is he talking about here? Did he actually say there's a system of Apartheid in Canada?" the answer is, of course, "yes." That would be the Indian Act, which still governs the everyday lives of Status Indians in Canada. It's a separate set of laws, applied only to one group of people, and based exclusively on race—the classic definition of Apartheid. If you find yourself having a hard time believing that your beloved country, which holds itself up as The Great Defender of Human Rights on the international stage, is the only western nation left with a system of Apartheid, well, you'll have to learn to deal with it. Better yet, get on the blower to your local MP and *do* something about it! Interesting, too, is the little-known fact that officials from South Africa visited Canada after World War II to see how Canadians "handled" their homeland peoples. And they learned a lot about how to do that by checking out Canada's *Indian Act.*

Here are a few tidbits: Why is it that Aboriginal people are expected to be "good Canadians" when they weren't allowed to vote in this country until 1960, and for many, many years weren't allowed to gather in groups off their reserves, couldn't leave their reserves without a pass, couldn't openly observe their own ways of praying and worshipping without being tossed in jail, and couldn't attend university or enter professional careers without losing their status as First Nations people? It can be a tough gig being a Native person in Canada. Just ask Perry. But we live with the hope that things are changing for the better.

Though the Apartheid treatment of Native people is really in your face once you *see* it (and it can be hard to see, given what your politicians and textbooks generally tell you), it's only the tip of the iceberg. How about this: why is it that two immigrant languages, English and French, are considered to be "official" languages in this country *now known* as Canada while the languages of the *original* people remain unrecognized and virtually unsupported by the Canadian government? Why is it that most non-Native Canadians expect Native people to be knowledgeable about *their* languages, *their* history, *their* traditions, *their* institutions, *their* justice system and *their* system of governance while most Canadians remain ignorant about Aboriginal languages, traditions, histories, institutions, justice systems and systems of governance? Shouldn't it be a two-way street? Why is it that western psychology, sociology, anthropology, medicine and perceptions of "reality" seem to be somehow superior to Native psychology, sociology, anthropology, medicine and perceptions of "reality"? Finally, why is it that the guests who came to this continent imposed *their* systems of thinking and governing on their hosts rather than accepting and adapting to existing Native systems of thinking and governing? In other words, why did the treaties with the British, French and then Canadian governments not do what they were supposed to do? The Aboriginal perspective on treaties is that they were (and are) spiritually based, land-sharing agreements made on a nation-to-nation basis for the purpose of creating a relationship of peaceful co-existence. So what the hell happened?

Whoa, Spielmann! Hold onto your proverbial horses for a minute! We don't want to get off to a bad start here by offending any non-Native types. The point is, we both have a lot that we can learn from each other about living together peacefully in this land and making this a great country for both Canadians and First Nations people. Heck, we might even become friends with each other some day. Wouldn't that be great? And that, basically, is what this book is about. Like the title says, it's meant to be a *survival guide* for Canadians who are increasingly realizing they still live in Anishnaabe World, but just aren't familiar with the social, cultural, political and spiritual landmarks. I mean, you don't really want the Canadian government to be the final arbiter of how to "fix" the mess we're in, do you? That would be like asking the Three Stooges to fix a leaky faucet. At the very least, you should come away from this book better informed about Aboriginal experience and how Anishnaabe people specifically see the world and their place in this country. And that can only help all of us.

A key motive for this book is my belief that many cross-cultural misunderstandings between people indigenous to this land now known as Canada and people with European ancestry arise from not knowing how to *interpret* the thinking and behavior of someone from a different culture. So, by focusing on examples of Native interactions which are seen as "peculiar" by many Canadians, and the cultural values underlying these interactions, I believe we can begin to come to a mutual understanding of and respect for each other. The guiding question for this survival guide then becomes: what *are* some of the basic cultural differences which so often lead to misunderstandings between Native people and Canadians, and how can these vast stretches of misunderstanding be bridged? That's what we want to try to figure out together.

And we really do need to figure it out. I mean, as I said earlier, it's not easy being Anishnaabe in this country now known as Canada. Half the non-Natives think you died off years ago (or should have, anyway), restaurant servers seem to drag their feet when waiting on your table, most of your traditional lands are open for business (but not open to you, anymore), and the non-Natives who belong to the Wannabe Tribe wonder why you don't wear those neat clothes like they did in *Dances With Wolves*. Worst of all, you have to put up with all of the ignorant questions (well, they're ignorant to most Native people, anyway) that most Canadians seem to have about "Indians," such as: "Why do Indians get everything free?" and, "Why can't you Indians quit your bitching and just learn to be good Canadians?" Another classic we've heard in various forms over the years goes something like this: "Why don't you Indians get off your asses and get jobs?" Like, first there have to be some jobs worth getting off one's ass for. Or, as one Canadian said to me recently, "Why don't those Indians just go back to where they came from?" Now that's an interesting idea... Sometimes it seems too bad that the value of kindness among Native people is so strong that it prohibits most Native people from shrugging their shoulders and responding to those kinds of questions with one of their own, like: "Why don't *you* just shut the fuck up?"

Uh, oh. Gotta calm down again. Breathe, Spielmann, breathe...in...out; and again, in...out... There...ok... Whew, a close one. Weird, I'm not even Anishnaabe. So, if even *I* get worked up about this stuff, maybe you can at least catch a fleeting glimpse of how it must be for Anishnaabe people. Even when they try to open the lines of communication, there are just so many obstacles impeding their right to a peaceful existence that panic and anger aren't far away. As I said, it ain't easy being Anishnaabe in "Canada." But, again, we live in hope. Let's get down to business.

An incident that occurred when I was living in the First Nation community of Pikogan clearly demonstrates some of the basic differences in thinking and doing things between Anishnaabe people and Canadians. Bush life is still an important part of everyday life for many people living in First Nation communities, particularly in many northern communities. Some families still live in the bush year-round and use their houses in the community as their "headquarters" when they come back from their bush camps and hunting grounds to go shopping for essential goods and to make contact with the rest of the community. People seem to feel more "at home" at their bush camps. It is a place where you can relax and be yourself without the hassles and frustrations that so often go along with life on the reserve. After all, most of the Elders spent more than half of their lives in traditional lifestyles: hunting, trapping, fishing and living their lives in the bush. The Elders were always so patient and kind with me, inviting me to go with them for moose hunting, beaver trapping and fishing. We would sit around the fire at night in summer or in a cozy cabin in winter and talk, drink tea, tell stories and laugh together. One of the Elders who had a great influence on my thinking and my life was Mr. Albert Mowatt (also known as Okinawe—pronounced "oh-**kin**-away"). He and his wife Anna often invited our family to go with them to the bush. Those times were very special for me and I learned so much about Native ways of thinking and living by listening and observing.

One summer I had a non-Native friend come and visit me. He's an avid fisherman and he asked me if Okinawe would take us fishing. I asked Okinawe and he agreed to take us. When we arrived at Okinawe's camp, the first thing we did was to get in his canoe and go set his nets out on the lake. My friend and I helped him set the nets and then we headed back to his cabin. As we were sitting together having tea, my friend asked me to ask Okinawe when we were going fishing. By this time I had started to catch on to what was happening, but I asked anyway:

"My friend wants to know when we're going fishing." Okinawe replied, "We just did." My friend was quite puzzled by this. He had brought his fishing rod with him, packed up in small carrying bag. He got it out, showed it to Okinawe and asked me to ask him where he could go fishing. Okinawe suggested that he could fish on the shore of the lake. So he did. I went down to the shore with him to watch. The shoreline was quite rocky and after awhile my friend had lost the lures he had brought with him. He asked me to ask Okinawe if he had any lures or hooks in his cabin. By this time I realized that there was a quite deep cultural gap coming into play in this situation, but I went ahead and asked Okinawe if he had any fishing hooks. He said he did and he came down to the shore with a huge gaffing hook; it looked like it was designed to catch a whale! The point is that Okinawe didn't have a concept of "sport fishing" or "sport

hunting." As he said to my friend later that evening over tea, "With a hook you can only catch one fish at a time. With a net you can catch lots of fish at one time." Lesson learned…

This experience with Okinawe provided me with a clue as to how different his thinking and ways of perceiving the world are from my own. The notion of sport fishing really didn't enter his conceptual world, just as Okinawe's understanding of fishing as just part of living didn't enter my friend's conceptual world. But my little story also shows something else. With regard to the cultural place accorded telling and listening to stories, too, there are subtle differences between Native people and non-Natives, generally speaking. It doesn't take one long, when hanging around Anishnaabe people, to discover that telling and listening to stories is much more conventionalized than in non-Native society. Certainly stories are used for entertainment, but more often than not there's a teaching about how to live a good life between the lines of the story. For now, the important thing to keep in mind is that when I'm telling you stories in this book, they're really tiny portals into the workings of the way Anishnaabe people think. In fact, as you read and interpret the anecdotes and episodes, you're acclimatizing to a new reality, which can be a heady, somewhat disorienting, experience. But I know you can handle it. You're smart people! Heck, you bought the book, right? You *gots* to have some smarts to take that kind of a chance!

2

Three Pretty Big Misconceptions

There are three main principles or "truths" regarding Anishnaabe people which I believe are fundamental to grasp if we are to begin to understand the importance of living together in peaceful co-existence in this country. Yet these truths are hidden behind longstanding *misconceptions* held by Canadians, so longstanding that they simply appear as reality to most non-Natives. Now you might want to hang on to your hats while we go through these; we might be about to experience a bit of vertigo-inducing turbulence. The first misconception is the most important one to straighten out because it takes us to the core of "who we are," be it Anishnaabe or Canadian. It goes something like this:

Three Pretty Big Misconceptions

1. We are all Canadians

...Actually, no, we're not. "What? Did this dude just tell us that we're not all Canadians who live in this great country of *Canada*? Like, is he really saying that Aboriginal people aren't Canadians? Then why don't they just go back to where they came from? I mean, love it or leave it, right?" Maybe now you can see what I mean when I encouraged you to hold on to your hats (and why I ended up in Canada just about the time the Vietnam War was starting to heat up...). A fruitful dialogue in this country between First Nations people and Canadians can only begin to occur when Canadians recognize that the vast majority of Aboriginal people in Canada today do *not* consider themselves *Canadian* in the same way that most Canadians do. When asked about their citizenship, virtually all Aboriginal people I know personally respond with the name of their First Nation. True, there seems to be some vague sense that they consider themselves "Canadian" insofar as they live in the geographical entity called Canada, but their primary identity is *not Canadian*, but *First Nation*. Makes sense, don't you think? Well, maybe not, yet. But until Canadians understand the basic fact that Aboriginal people *do not* primarily consider themselves to be Canadians, the walls of ignorance and misunderstanding will continue to exist; the chances of a two-way street of acceptance will be slim. But my guess is that you guys are smart enough to see that it makes pretty much common sense that a Native person's first allegiance is not to Canada, but to her or his own First Nation. Wouldn't you feel the same? C'mon now, wouldn't you? I thought so...

The second misconception also relates to identity:

2. First Nations people are an "ethnic group"

Surprise! They're not. I don't know how many times over the years this issue has come up with Canadian politicians and Canadian citizens. It shows a real misunderstanding that most Canadians have about Native people. It is most commonly expressed along the following lines: "Well, if we let Indians have their own schools and let them make their own laws in their own communities, what about the Italians and Greeks and Chinese, etc., etc." Or, "Shouldn't First Nations people be like every everyone else in Canada and drop all that 'Indian stuff' and just learn to become good Canadians?" Hmm...Let me say this as clearly as possible: by nature of being indigenous people (indigenous referring to where a people originates), they cannot be viewed as an "ethnic group" (which assumes they originally came from "somewhere else" outside of North America). And, yes, First Nations *ought* to have their own schools and *ought* to be able to create their own laws in their own territories precisely because they are *not* mere ethnic groups but are indigenous to this land; not to mention (yet, anyway) that these Aboriginal Rights are enshrined in every treaty in Canada, as well as in Canada's own Charter of Rights. But we'll come back to that issue in due course. And, no, Italian immigrants and Greek immigrants and any others with immigrant backgrounds, that is non-indigenous backgrounds, do not have the right to their own schools or to make their own laws (unless they're willing to pay for their own schools themselves). By virtue of immigrating to this country of Canada, people coming to Canada from other parts of the world pledge to follow Canadian laws and participate, as much as possible, in Canadian culture, including learning English or French and going to Canadian schools. And rightfully so. I mean, that's basically what *your* ancestors did, right? And, let's say you decide to move to Mexico, wouldn't you feel that it is your obligation to become acculturated and learn to speak Spanish and learn about Mexican history and governance and Mexican laws? Sure! Just makes sense, right? But, unless you were born in Mexico and you were a Mexican citizen, certainly you would agree that you do not have an inherent right to do whatever you like, as you did in your "home" country, right? But Indigenous people, by right of being indigenous to this land, *do* have this right.

3. All First Nations in Canada are the same

Now, it probably shouldn't come as much of a surprise, given the presentation of First Nations people in the various media and in Canadian history books until fairly recently, and given misconception # 2, but many Canadians harbour the false assumption that there exists only one homogeneous First Nation in Canada, speaking the same language and pretty much thinking and doing things the same way. Nothing could be further from the truth. The fact is, there are eleven distinct language families in Canada today, comprising 53 distinct Aboriginal languages. "Come again?" Yeah, 53 *distinct* Aboriginal languages. Each language is unique and has its own set of grammars, lexical items, rules of use, and so on. Most languages in different language families are mutually unintelligible, meaning that an Aboriginal person who speaks a language from one language family (the Athabaskan family, say) would not likely be able to communicate with an Aboriginal person from a different language family (the Algonquian family, for example). And then, of course, each language has a multitude of dialects, which makes the linguistic landscape extremely rich and complex—not to mention confusing! But hey, it's not like you need to *learn* all these languages. I just think you need to be aware that the tendency of Canadian attitudes towards First Nations until recently (and I *do* think things are beginning to change) had the effect of reducing them to a superficial stereo-type. Now, *you* don't like being considered superficial, right? Well... So, ok, now that I've massaged that stereotype out of you (better than beating it out, wouldn't you say?), you're ready to get down to the reality of Aboriginal experience in Canada.

Anyway, where were we? Oh, yeah! In a nutshell, this book is mainly written for non-Native Canadians who are pretty much uninformed about Native ways of thinking and doing things. So, in the next chapter let's go back to a few of the basic questions we started off with in this book, so as not to lose our way. With a little luck, by the end of the book the Anishnaabe reader will be thinking, "Yep, that's what non-Native Canadians need to know if we're gonna have mutual respect in this country." And the Canadian reader will think, "Yep, I didn't really know any of this stuff before I read this book. It was worth the $18.95..." Something like that, anyway.

3

The Big Questions
and How to Make Sense of Them

Okay, here's the chapter we've *really* all been waiting for! In this chapter I want to start to get down and dirty by trying to reproduce, and then offer logical answers to, the daily questions most Anishnaabe people get from Canadians that tend to reveal how little most non-Native Canadians know about their own country and its history, including its relationship with First Nations people. But, hey, we're looking forward to answering some of the BIG questions. In fact, I have our mailbag right here in front of us, so how about you go rummaging through the mail, Perry, and we'll answer as many questions as we can, or at least start to answer them. They do get quite complicated at times...

So, where to start? Hey, here's a good one that we hear just about every day! It goes something like this:

1. How Come Indians Get Free Education?

Ah! If only I had a nickel for every time I've heard that question. The deeper issue is, of course, how come they get free education and we Canadians don't! Okay, let's jump in and see if we can do a little eddicatin' here!

First, it's important to understand the relationship that has developed between the Canadian government and First Nations ever since confederation (even before confederation, really). When Europeans first landed on the shores of what First Nations commonly refer to as "Turtle Island," their eyes lit up! "Hey, look at all this neat stuff! Lots of fertile land, trees— hell, I bet there's gold in them there hills!" Well, you get the picture. The only bothersome thing was that there were already people living here, although at first contact the Catholic Church back in Europe couldn't decide if they were "humans" or "critters." If they were just "critters," then, heck, you could just kill 'em off like you would any other critter. But if they were "human," meaning they possessed "souls," well, that would present the newcomers with a different problem. So, after about 40 years of debate (things like "making decisions" tend to move a bit, shall we say, *slowly* in the Catholic Church…), the Church finally decided (around 1537) that, for better or for worse, these creatures found in this so-called "New World" were, indeed, human, and thus had souls and thus had to be missionized and civilized (rather than merely slaughtered). Turned out to be good news for the people indigenous to this land!

The short version of the story, which leads us back to our original question, is that a process for living together peacefully on this land was born—that being the *"treaty-making"* process. Now, while still more than half of this country now known as Canada is not covered by treaties with the original inhabitants, a number of treaties have been struck with various First Nations. And in every one of those treaties there is a promise by the Canadian government to provide "education" to all First Nations people. What do the First Nations people have to do? Simply "cede, release, surrender and yield up to the government of the Dominion of Canada, for His Majesty the King and His successors for ever, all their rights, titles and privileges what-soever, to the lands" (from *Treaty 9*) indicated in the respective treaty, namely, all their traditional lands. Good deal, eh? Virtually all Canada's forestry, hydro electric, and mineral resources come from these lands the Native peoples "surrendered" to the Crown. Get it? *Crown Land.* There's a teensy problem here though, in the fact that the Aboriginal people had no concept of *ownership.* They saw themselves as *using* the land the creator had provided, and if they could use it, well, surely the white folks could too. They'd *share* the land. That way both groups could live together peacefully. But here is where things get a bit dicey. Of course these different cultural understandings—sharing and ownership—have led to the current web of land claims and treaty negotiations we are now tangled in.

We'll return to the treaty-making process in chapter twelve, but for now the basic deal is this: in exchange for our (Canadian) use of the land (and all the money we can make from it! Ka-Ching!), we promised in the treaties to fund all First Nations educational needs. Now, it seems pretty simple, don't you think? You agree to share a portion of your traditional territories in exchange for "education," right? The problem is the Canadian Government has fallen far short of—when not outright welching on—its part of the bargain to provide Aboriginal people with that so-called "free education"! That's right—*your* Canadian history books aren't quite telling you the whole truth. I mean, actions speak louder than words, right? To make matters more laughable (gotta laugh folks, gotta laugh…), now that the federal government has sloughed off all the education respon-sibilities for First Nation students who don't live on a reserve or on Crown Land onto the provinces, those original obligations for education have turned into the proverbial hot potato, with each level of government trying to get it out of their hands as fast as possible! Bet you never read about *that* in your history books! One teensy example: studies indicate (doncha just love that phrase, especially when it works for ya?) that federally funded on-reserve schools receive between 20% and 40% less funding than provincially funded off-reserve schools of equivalent size. (See studies by Matthew and Postl, online at www.fnesc.ca.) No wonder the provinces don't want to pay for reserve schools. And one has to wonder if the feds are still in the educate-to-assimilate business (see the next question, below), except now the strategy is attrition—underfund them and they will leave the reserve. *Voila!* Problem of paying for education solved.

Anyway, the point is the whole concept of "free" education has *never* been true, unless you consider getting huge chunks of land in exchange for providing partial education to Native people as "free." But, hey, you can't have your cake and eat it, too (try as you might). And it seems the governments are still trying: in

Being Nish is sure full of wonderful FREE stuff eh?...
...free poverty, free diabetes, free mortality rates...!

recent decades, the provinces have unilaterally (which means without negotiation or consultation with the First Nations affected) decided to put a "cap" on the money to be spent by each Native community for potential, and eligible, Anishnaabe students to study off-reserve in the provincial system, thus pretty much nullifying the whole misconception of "free" education. After all, almost every Anishnaabe community has a lengthy list of students eligible to attend college and university but who can't go because there's no money available to them! At least, according to what the provincial Ministers of Education keep saying—if *they* can be believed. But, of course, the province continues to make tons of money each year from resources that are extracted from what *used to be* traditional Anishnaabe territories.

So how about a compromise here, seeing as how the provinces keep saying that they can't afford to keep up their end of the bargain: why not just give all the land back to the First Nations and you won't have to provide them with *anything*, including this so-called "free" education. Oh, and don't worry about where you might have to live and work—I'm sure the First Nations will be only be too happy to provide you with tiny pockets of reserve land, box houses and all. You might not have any sewer systems or running water, but, hey, at least you won't be giving First Nations "free" education.

Next question, please?

2. Why Do Those Indians Keep Complaining About Residential Schools?

Hey, this question follows the last one perfectly! Okay, you've likely all heard the maxim: "You can't understand another person until you've walked a mile in his or her moccasins." Well, let's put those moccasins on and walk that proverbial mile and see how we feel.

Needless to say, there was a drastic misunderstanding in the signing of the treaties. Not only did the Anishnaabe think they were sharing land rather than surrendering it, they also couldn't have known what the government meant by *education*. I mean, put yourself in their moccasins. Would you have agreed to sign a document if you'd known that the author of it, Duncan Campbell Scott, was using education as an instrument of assimilation? Listen to him in 1920, as the Deputy Super-intendent of Indian Affairs: "Education is the answer to the Indian problem—education, education until there is no Indian left" (in Milloy 39). "I want to get rid of the Indian problem. ... Our objective is to continue until there is not a single Indian in Canada who has not been absorbed into the body politic and there is no Indian question and no Indian problem" (in Milloy 46).

The strategy was to use education to christianize and civilize the raggedy savages. The residential schools were the means. For over 100 years the government turned the education of all

Aboriginal children in Canada over to the churches. Hmm…the churches? To educate First Nations children? You think I'm kidding, right? Uh, no. All churches: Catholic, Presbyterian, Anglican, United, and so forth, took part in this great plan…

So, without consulting the First Nations people (yet again), the Canadian government entered into the kidnapping business. By the way, if you think I'm just making this stuff up, maybe you should turn off the classic rock station and, like, read the paper, or listen to CBC radio… I mean the government even formally *apologized* for the residential school system in 2008! Listen to this, from Prime Minister Stephen Harper, June 11, 2008:

> I stand before you today to offer an apology to former students of Indian residential schools. The treatment of children in these schools is a sad chapter in our history. For more than a century, Indian Residential Schools separated over 150,000 Aboriginal children from their families and communities. In the 1870's, the federal government, partly in order to meet its obligation to educate Aboriginal children, began to play a role in the development and administration of these schools.

> Two primary objectives of the Residential Schools system were to remove and isolate children from the influence of their homes, families, traditions and

cultures, and to assimilate them into the dominant culture. These objectives were based on the assumption Aboriginal cultures and spiritual beliefs were inferior and unequal. Indeed, some sought, as it was infamously said, "to kill the Indian in the child". Today, we recognize that this policy of assimilation was wrong, has caused great harm, and has no place in our country.

But they did last in Canada from the 1870s until the last one was mercifully closed down in 1986. And what happened at these residential schools? Well, to be fair, atrocities weren't committed at *every* residential school, just the majority of them. What kinds of atrocities, you ask? Ah, where to begin? First, all Aboriginal kids of school age were forcibly scooped up and taken out of their communities to be sent to one of the dozens of residential schools scattered across the country. Any Aboriginal parents who tried to stop this kidnapping or tried to hide their children were tossed into prison. First Nations were beginning to learn a very hard lesson when dealing with white people: don't mess with them. They had all the power, and, as we've learned many times from a multitude of historical experiences around the world, the ones with the power make the rules.

Back to the atrocities. In 1990 Phil Fontaine, at this writing the National Chief of the Assembly of First Nations (AFN), found the courage to go public with his experience in the residential school he was forced to attend when he was a child. He talked openly to the Canadian public about being sexually and physically abused by the priests and nuns who ran the school he was forced to attend. He talked about how he and his friends were beaten if they were caught speaking their Native language to each other. And that was just the tip of the iceberg…

My residential school teacher was so mean…
They took the "O" out of her "Obituary"!!

The floodgates opened. As soon as Phil Fontaine went public with Canada's dirty little secret about what was really happening at these residential schools, other abused residential school survivors began to tell their stories—again, the ones who survived… First dozens, then hundreds, then thousands upon thousands of First Nations people went public with their stories. Within a few short years, Canada, who prided itself on being a "Defender of Human Rights" on the international scene, began to be seen as a joke. No longer the nice, passive, humane Canada was seen, but the reality of a brutal, inhumane, vicious, and yes, cowardly, nation was in the international spotlight. And they didn't like it one damn bit!

By 1995, the nation of Canada had been condemned by virtually every human rights organization in the world, including the United Nations, for their "inhumane and unconscionable" treatment of "their" indigenous people (Tobias, 2003; Steckley and Cummins, 2006). A new chapter was beginning for First Nations in Canada: a chapter of healing and restitution, which continues to this day. A mere few weeks prior to this writing (in April, 2009), the Catholic Church, led by Pope Ratzinger (no jokes about his last name, please—it wasn't his fault), finally offered an official apology for all of the abuses committed by its clergy and lay members for their treatment of indigenous people around the world, with particular emphasis on their mistreatment of First Nations people in Canada. Finally.

Now, here we are getting pretty serious about this whole "Survival Guide" for Canadians thing when we wanted to keep it light and entertaining. But some things just can't be treated with kid gloves, and this is one of them. We'd like to add a bit of a footnote here. I have been asked by many, many Canadians over the years "Why should I feel guilty about what happened in the past?" After all, they didn't run the residential schools and, heck, they even like Indians! And you know: they're right. But here's how I usually respond when I'm asked the question: "You're right. I don't blame you personally, and you shouldn't feel guilty about the past, *but if you don't educate yourself about Native issues in the next decade, then you will become part of the problem and you should feel guilty.* It's up to you: do you want a strong, multicultural Canada, or a country that treats its own citizens as if they live in a fourth-world country?" It's up to you.

Spanish Indian Residential School

3. Why Don't Indians Pay Taxes?

Hey, did you ever play that game where everyone sits in a circle and one person whispers a sentence into the ear of the person next to him or her, and so on around the circle, until the last person says the sentence aloud and it comes out completely different? Weird, eh? Well, imagine a big group of Canadians sitting in a circle stretching from sea to sea to sea. The first person whispers the following sentence into the next person's ear: "Native people are exempt from paying Canadian taxes under certain special circumstances." Round and round and round it goes. How it comes out, nobody knows… Uh, wrong. We all know how it comes out: "Indians don't pay any taxes in Canada!" Followed by the standard indignant question: *"Why not?"* I've heard that question so many times I've lost count. Somehow, it seems to make people feel better to base their understanding on parlour games. Or half-truths. Or quarter-truths. Or even $1/10^{th}$ truths. Because it's about $1/10^{th}$ true that Native People don't pay taxes. Ok, here's the deal. Ready? Get out your steno pads and take a memo, to yourselves. In relation to income tax, the fact is more than 90% of First Nations people *do* pay income tax. The *only* exemption—applying to less than 10% of the Native work force in Canada—is if you work on a reserve or in an Aboriginal organization. For example, one of my colleague's spouses works at Vale Inco, the nickel mining company in Sudbury. He pays income tax, year in and year out. My colleague at the University of Sudbury, too, pays income tax, year in and year out. Get it? They don't work on a reserve!

And as for permitting Native people who do work on a reserve not to pay income tax, well, guess whose idea that was? Canada's. It's right there in Section 87 of the Indian Act (1876):

87.

   (1) Notwithstanding any other Act of Parliament or any Act of the legislature of a province ... the following property is exempt from taxation:

   (*a*) the interest of an Indian or a band in reserve lands or surrendered lands; and

   (*b*) the personal property of an Indian or a band situated on a reserve.

   (2) No Indian or band is subject to taxation in respect of the ownership, occupation, possession or use of any property mentioned in paragraph (1)(*a*) or (*b*) or is otherwise subject to taxation in respect of any such property.

There it is: as an "Indian" your income is "personal property," and is therefore exempt from tax, if you or the band paying you are situated on a reserve.

"Yeah, well what about the GST? I've seen Native people whip out a status card at a store nowhere near a reserve, and they don't have to pay the tax. What gives?" Good eye! Me, I just nod off in checkout lines. But okay. The situation is actually similar to the income tax exemption. The goods and services Anishnaabe people purchase off reserve are their *property*, and are therefore exempt from GST, *if,* wait for it:

- they have the appropriate documentation to show the vendor [i.e. a status card]; and
- the goods are delivered *to a reserve* by the vendor or the vendor's agent. [italics mine]

(from the Canada Revenue Agency website)

So, card-carrying status Indians who work on reserves or buy stuff to be used on reserves are exempt from GST. Again, less than 10% of First Nations people in Canada. And there you have it. Another misconception clarified! Don't you feel *good?*

4. Why Don't Indians Just Become Good Canadians Like The Rest Of Us?

Still got those moccasins on? Okay, good. Let's do a bit of self-checking. Ask yourself how you'd feel if you were a Native parent and the federal government came to your community and forcibly took your six school-age kids hundreds of miles away to be "educated" without your consent (threatening to toss you in jail if you protested)? Well, I'm gonna go out on a bit of a limb here and try to guess how you might feel: *pretty goddamed pissed off!* Of course, that's just a guess... But consider the consequences faced by First Nation parents and communities. The children who were forcibly taken from their families and communities to attend residential schools were often sexually and physically abused by their so-called "caretakers" and teachers, including the clergy; were physically punished for speaking their own languages, and often wouldn't see their families or communities for years at a time. True, not all residential schools were the same, but the general consensus is that most of them fall into this category of being places of abuse and dehumanization. And death.

Then when they finally did make it back home to their families, they couldn't speak with their own parents because they had lost their languages (or had them beaten out of them), they had been ripped away from their communities and Elders, including their traditional teachings, spiritual beliefs and practices, and almost everything "Aboriginal." Many have said over the past twenty years that they felt like strangers in their own families and communities. They felt like white people.

Those moccasins starting to chafe a bit? Okay, now the question becomes: "How would you feel towards Canada, churches and white people?" Let's try a bit more guesswork. I bet that you would feel pretty much the same way that Aboriginal people today feel about what happened. You'd definitely want to give them all Sweeney Todd haircuts! Okay, we're pretty sure the publisher won't allow that, so let's put it this way: You'd be pretty angry, and hurt, and feel pretty marginalized and lost. And if you're a parent, those feelings would be multiplied. We don't know how else to put it, so we'll leave the final words to the Cree author and playwright Tomson Highway. As Highway relates his life experiences about growing up on a remote reserve in Manitoba and his experiences during his residential school days, we are drawn into the dark pool of real life experiences that form the basis of his works. In *Dry Lips Oughta Move to Kapuskasing* he writes: "Before the healing can take place, the poison must first be exposed."

Finally…

5. Why Do You Keep Saying That Canada Is The Only Western Country In The World With A System Of Apartheid?

Oh, gentle reader, how I would love to hold your hand and take you merrily down the path of Canadian History and tell you what a wonderful, racist-free, Apartheid-free country you live in! But there's one problem.

The Big Questions

YOU DON'T LIVE THERE!

And the sooner you figure that out, that your government officials have been foisting lie upon lie on you for decades, the better chance we *all* have to collaboratively create a country that we can all be proud of, both First Nations people and Canadians.

So, here's your chance—your "kicking off the mocassins" point, so to speak. Either you do your homework and find out what the truth is—which is what I've been telling you all along—or close this book and toss it into the fireplace. If you're happy living in Never-Never Land, then I suggest that you continue to do just that. And why not pop a handful of Prozac while you're at it…

Now wait just a minute Spielmann! Isn't that a bit over the top, again? Yeah, yeah, it's your conscience talking! Deal with it Roger! You know you hate the "my way or the highway" rhetoric. That's why you're writing this book, after all. Isn't it true you think most Canadians will want to set up a "right" relationship with Anishnaabe people? Haven't you been saying that's your hope? Huh? Yeah, I thought you'd agree. Okay. You seem to be calming down again. I'm outta here (but remember, I'm listening…).

Whew, that was weird! But okay, if you're the type of person I think most Canadians are, people strong enough to handle the truth about this so-called great country of theirs, and who want to do something to make it better, then I encourage you to keep reading.

With the recent move in South Africa towards the dismantling of the system of Apartheid, Canada is the only country left in the western world where such a system still exists. With its legislated system of separation by race as embodied in the *Indian Act*, Canada continues to promote a racist (...a "legislated system of separation by race." Am I lying?) and paternalistic relationship with First Nations. As far as Aboriginal people are concerned, that relationship is about to end. A new relationship will be established, with or without the "consent" of the Canadian government and the Canadian people. First Nations are not asking to be "given" anything. They are asking that their inherent right to manage their own affairs be recognized.

There is a sense of optimism among First Nations as they go about the business of regaining control over their affairs and communities. In the twenty-first century, for the first time, the Canadian government is beginning to talk not in terms of "giving" First Nations anything, but rather of recognizing what they believe has existed and continues to exist since contact: the inherent right to govern themselves in their own territories. One example:

The Province of B.C., the First Nations Education Steering Committee and Canada signed the Education Jurisdiction Framework Agreement in July 2006. Through this agreement, and subsequent federal enabling legislation, Canada has recognized First Nations' power to make laws over education on their own lands. B.C.'s legislation formally recognizes that right and enables boards of education and independent schools to enter into education agreements with participating First Nations. (Joint 2007 News Release of the First Nations Education Steering Committee and the BC Ministry of Education; http://www2. news.gov.bc.ca/news_releases_2005-2009/ 2007EDU0161-001500.htm)

So maybe, just maybe, there's hope for this country called *Canada* to become a truly great country. But we just ain't there yet...

4

A "Gentle" Letter-Writer
Gets a Tour of the Rez

In light of William Thomas's column "From the Land of the Loony," about how uninformed most Canadians still are about history in general (2007), I thought I'd share some excerpts from a letter I received a while back chastising me for writing a column about First Nations issues in the *Sudbury Star*. As the letter-writer stated, "If you won't admit it to the general public, you should at least admit to yourself that the Indian is *one hundred times better off today* than he ever would have been if left to his own devices."

Hmm...*that* caught my attention. My column was about how most Native people are pretty hip to non-Native ways of thinking and doing things, but how ignorant and misinformed most Canadians still are about *Aboriginal* ways of thinking and doing things. For example, most Native people know how to speak one of the so-called "official" languages in Canada, have gone through the Canadian educational system, and know quite a bit about Canadian history. But how many non-Natives in Canada know how to speak a Native language? Or know anything about Native history? Anyway, that was the gist of the column. The letter-writer went on to say, "Shame on you! You and I both know that when our ancestors arrived here the Indian was running around with a pointed stick for a weapon, trying to eke out a living when he wasn't busy stabbing his enemies in the eye with it." (*Note to self*: Is that the "pointy-stick" theory of how First Nations people survived in North America for thousands of years prior to European contact? I wonder...). The letter-writer continued by saying, "Had we arrived on the scene a few years later, the Indian population would probably have self-destructed by then."

Kind of scary encountering such a confident tone of righteousness wrapped around blatant ignorance. Especially when you consider the fact that the consensus of historians who study populations estimates that there were between 75 and 125 million indigenous people in the Americas in 1492 (Churchill, 2001; Lipstadt, 1993; Hobsbawm, 1983). (Even my publisher raised his eyebrows when he read that "...even the most conservative estimates put the indigenous population in the Americas at 75 million or so at the beginning of the 15th century, and now it's down to around ten million" (Dobyns, 1966:4).) In fact, Aboriginal people, while horrified by the Holocaust of the Jews in World War II, often comment on how so little is known about the massive holocaust of *indigenous* people in the Americas over the relatively small historical period of 500 years. It bears repeating: the most conservative estimates of the indigenous population accepted by bi-partisan historians is around 75 million, with other historians putting the number at 125 million. However you look at it, that's a holocaust of major proportions by anyone's standards, wouldn't you agree? But that's an altogether different book.

Clearly it escaped the letter-writer that such population diminishment happened AFTER the arrival of Europeans on this soil. Our letter-writing friend continued, "There is not enough room in one letter to list all the undeserved perks, privileges and advantages the Indian enjoys over and above that which any tax-paying white citizens could ever even hope for." Finally, our epistolary pal concludes by saying, "The sorriest part of this whole Indian situation is that the media, along with irresponsible do-gooders like yourself, are allowed to run around free and perpetuate the timeworn myth that the Indian is still being abused. No doubt it makes good reading for the uninformed city-dwelling public and allows your Indian friends to continue sitting on their duffs on the totally taxpayer-subsidized reserves where they are free to spend their time hunting and fishing like a bunch of retired millionaires."

Actually the guy is onto something about the media perpetuating myths, but the something is not quite what he thinks it is. As the shelved, $56,000,000.00, Royal Commission on Aboriginal Peoples put it, "Aboriginal people are not well-represented by or in the media. Many Canadians know Aboriginal people only as noble environmentalists, angry warriors or pitiful victims. A full picture of their humanity is simply not available in the media. Mainstream media do not reflect Aboriginal realities very well. Nor do they offer much space to Aboriginal peoples to tell their own stories."

While I appreciate the reference to being a "do-gooder" (as opposed to being an "evil-doer" maybe?), I'm not really sure what to say to our letter-writer other than: GET A LIFE! But, all kidding aside, we would encourage people who care about this nation of Canada to inform themselves about Canadian history and the real story behind the dysfunctional relationship between First Nations people and Canadians. Heck, you might even want to visit a reserve and ask some *real* Anishnaabe about their contribution to Canadian history. That is, if you can find anyone who's not out hunting and fishing like some retired millionaire...

After receiving such a bizarre response to my *Sudbury Star* article, I started thinking, "I wonder what I would say to this person if I had the opportunity to speak with him face-to-face?" I think, if possible, I would invite him (and any other interested Canadians) to visit a real reserve in order to see what it's like. Maybe that would help defuse some of our timeworn stereotypes and misconceptions, I thought. In the meantime, how about working your imagination a bit? Let's visit a reserve right here in these pages. Call it a "virtual tour" and we can feel high tech...

Recently I read this neat book called *Long Shadows: Truth, Lies and History*, written by Erna Paris. One part of the book explores the (now-dismantled) South African system of Apartheid, modeled, as said earlier, after the *Indian Act* in Canada. In both countries "reserves" were established where indigenous (or homeland) people were strenuously encouraged and even forced to live. I mean, how else could one get the homeland people out of the way of "civilization" (read: land + resources = lots of money)? While reserves no longer exist in South Africa, they still exist in Canada and many of these reserves have now become "home communities" to many First Nations people. But what's life REALLY like on the rez? Every reserve is different; some are pretty cool places and others, especially in the far north, are not so cool. Just about everyone has heard stuff in the media about reserve life, and usually these media portraits are pretty bleak. For the rest of this chapter, then, I want to provide you with a visitor's guide to these uncharted territories, a wilderness guide for the adventurous traveler, the self-righteous but ignorant letter-writer, the hardy Shognosh (non-Native) who wishes to explore the Great Mystery of Indian life on the reserve. Don your buckskins, pack your peace pipe, lace up your all-weather moccasins...hey, wait! I'm just kidding! C'mon now, don't go all "Grey Owl" on me! (Note: Remember Grey Owl?—kind of represents somebody acting like a loveable, wannabe dork...).

Preparing for Your Trip

Before you leave for your visit to the reserve, be sure and let some close friends and relatives know where, exactly, you're going. That way, authorities will know how to notify your next-of-kin (just in case). Tell them that if you don't return within a week or so that you've either been seriously, well, killed, or that you've fallen in love with a beautiful Anishnaabe princess (or prince) and you're now happily living the rest of your life as a member of the Wannabe Tribe. Believe me, it may sound like a fairy tale, but one might be surprised by how often such situations have actually occurred! And, to be fair, early on in the history of relations between Native people and European-based peoples, a whole nation was born, the Métis nation, due to the number of marriages between Aboriginal people and the Europeans. They also had a somewhat difficult relationship with the Canadian government. Again, you may have trouble finding the full story in your Canadian history books…but have a look, under Riel Rebellion.

Medical Advice

Be sure to have any major surgery done before you go. A lot has been said about Canada's health-care system and how Native people get everything free, but the reality of the situation is a bit different in most Native communities, at least the ones in the north. At all costs you'll want to avoid any serious medical problems which may require hospitalization—unless it's something that can survive a three-day trip by canoe without dire consequences.

One thing I should note, though, in this section on "medical advice." If you don't smoke, now might be a good time to *start*

We thought we would save them some time!

A Tour of the Rez

… You'll feel like you're really fitting in and, after all, tobacco *is* considered to be a sacred herb in Anishnaabe World. Not that it's necessarily being *used* as a sacred herb when you're just out having a smoke, but the thought is there… In fact, a buddy of mine told me about a non-smoking Sudbury psychiatrist who used to carry a few packs of cigarettes in his glove box for the Elders on the reserves he visited. He was well-loved! Interesting, too, how tobacco can be used to mend broken friendships and relationships. I remember one time a friend of mine on the rez where I used to live asked me to drive him to a friend's house— he'd had an argument with the person a few days earlier and he wanted to "make amends" and be friends again. So I took him there, waited in my car for about ten minutes, and he came out holding a lit cigarette. I didn't say anything to him right away, but I knew he was a non-smoker, so when we were out of sight of his friend's house, I asked him, "What the hell are you doing smoking?" He threw the cigarette out of the car, turned to me and said, "Well, I wanted to restore our friendship, so I walked in [as is the custom on the rez—nobody knocks or rings the doorbell—not that there are any doorbells to ring anyway!], and we had some tea together. We never brought up the situation that had come between our friendship. We just talked. Then, as I was leaving, he offered me a cigarette. He knows I don't smoke, but I took it anyway, knowing that he was actually saying that he wanted to be friends again, too." Kind of a long explanation for such a seemingly simple gesture, but I think you can see the complexity and richness of it as well.

From that point on I started seeing tobacco used in this way many times, and even started using it myself. One time I had a disagreement with an Elder over something (I even forget what now) and I wanted to renew our friendship, so I went to his house, walked in, had some tea and we talked, never mentioning whatever it was that had come between us. As I got up to leave he said, "That was a nice talk." Then he flipped me a cigarette and said, "You're forgiven!" Even more interesting is that there is no word for "forgiveness" in the Anishnaabe language, which tends to drive white people nuts! "Those Indians are so rude; they never apologize or ask for forgiveness!" Like, first you need a *word* for "apologize" or "forgive." But most important, it's crucial to understand how things are done in a different culture and to act accordingly when with the people of that culture, don't you think?

How to Get There

This is not an easy one to handle. Like, sure, you can look on a map and pinpoint some reserve and then try to follow the map to get there, but did you ever see the movie *Apocalypse Now*? We're not saying that it's difficult to physically find an Indian reserve—that's the easy part—but we can pretty much guarantee that your impression of what you've stumbled into will be just about as disoriented as when Martin Sheen finally found Capt. Kurtz in the movie. The best advice we have to offer is that you try and find some Nish (Native person) and see if you can wangle an invitation back to their community. Kind of like hiring a guide...

When to Go

Most First Nation reserves are pretty much open all year round. About the only bad time to visit would be during moose-hunting season or beaver-trapping season, at least in many of the northern communities when everyone's in the bush. Oh, yes, and most holidays. Heck, you know how irritating it is to have people drop in on you unannounced during holidays. You already own most of these peoples' traditional lands, so now you want to "drop in" for a visit during the holidays? I don't think so...

Customs and Immigration

Surprise! You don't have to pass through customs or immigration to visit an Indian reserve in Canada. You should have to, of course, but most Anishnaabe people don't have as much power over their lives and communities as they did for thousands and thousands of years before your ancestors got lost and accidentally "discovered" this continent and totally messed up their lives... But I digress.

Fitting In

Before actually setting foot on a real reserve, we would advise you to familiarize yourself with some of the cultural traditions, customs and values so that you don't so easily appear to be what you really are. Like, you at least want to pretend that you're trying to fit in, right? So here are a couple of helpful hints to enable you to better blend into the reserve landscape and not stick out like a sore thumb.

Be yourself—which may not be all that simple since we all have a tendency as human beings to put on our particular "persona." The point here is that you're going to stick out like a sore thumb anyways (regardless of what we just said...), so you're better off just being yourself and not trying to pretend that (a) you're an Indian, or (b) that you're a know-it-all white person.

Be prepared for the unexpected—When my wife and I first entered the community of Pikogan, it felt as if we were on a different planet at times! Almost like "Bizarro World" in the Superman comics where everything seems upside down. For example, when my wife's father passed away and she had been away from the community for a month, one of the Elders, a close friend, came up to my wife when we returned and said with a big smile (and in front of a lot of other people), *"Oh, gigichi aajiboonan!"* which means, "Oh, you're so fat!" Now, in non-Native culture that's not much of a compliment! In fact, you would rarely, if *ever*, say something like that to someone unless you were trying to hurt that person's feelings. But in this instance, it was offered as a *compliment*. The Elder had been concerned that my wife would not be eating enough while mourning and would return to the community looking thin and unhealthy. In *her* culture, people who have plenty of meat on their bones are considered healthy and strong. Part of the reason for this goes back to when people were living traditional lifestyles in the bush, as most of the Elders at Pikogan had done for over half of their lives. It was always important to have plenty of extra meat on your bones to tide you through when game was scarce and food not readily available. Such a value remains strong even though most people don't live exclusively in the bush anymore. Of course, after my wife received this compliment she immediately went on a diet! But the point is that what is considered to be a *rude* thing to do or say in one culture may be the conventionally *polite* thing to do or say in another, and understanding the values underlying appropriate interaction can go a long way in easing cross-cultural confusion and misunderstanding.

A little language goes a long way—As for the unexpected, if you learn just a little of the language before you go on your visit, and maybe a few cultural ways of doing things, well, that can take you a long way to being accepted. Especially language. Just knowing how to say *"Aanii! Aanishnaa!"* ("Hi! How's it going?") will put a big smile on the faces of the Elders (and others, too!).

Believe me, you're going to be taken by surprise a number of times during your visit, so be ready for it. Despite what many non-Native types tend to think, Native people really are fueled by a different set of values and traditions, which makes for a different way of thinking and doing things. And these different ways of thinking and doing things are much more noticeable on the reserve than off it. Keep in mind that you're the guest—not the boss, and certainly not the "know-it-all" white guy! So, enjoy yourself; you might even learn something from people who have lived in these parts for a helluva long time.

5

Some Basic Value Differences Between Canadians And First Nations

Back in Chapter three I responded to a common question put by non-Anishnaabe people: "Why don't Indians just learn to be good Canadians? Wouldn't that make Canada a better country?" My response there related to residential schools and the treaties, and was, possibly, a might *testy*. Here I want to change tack. In the next few paragraphs I'll focus on the richness and complexity of Anishnaabe-specific ways of thinking, doing things and relating to the world around us, which would also be abandoned and eventually lost forever under such a scenario of "everyone being a good Canadian."

Granted, it's a bit difficult to make all-encompassing observations and generalizations about "Anishnaabe-specific" ways of thinking and doing things due to the tremendous variety of Anishnaabe traditions and experiences in Canada today. Remember Canadian misconception #3, that there exists One Indian Nation in Canada. Nothing could be further from the truth. Anishnaabe Nations, experiences, beliefs, languages, and so on, express tremendous cultural variety.

Despite all the variety, though, there is a deep and entrenched value in the Anishnaabe community which even most non-Anishnaabe people have at least heard about: the value of *respect*. Anishnaabe people have a very deep feeling that one's life and experience is meant to be just the way it is. *Kije Manido*, the Great Spirit, has a purpose for each individual, creature, natural phenomenon and event. Nothing happens apart from this design. From this fundamental respect flow all the other cultural manifestations that can surprise and irritate Canadians. Let's have a look at some, and highlight how they differ from Canadian cultural practices.

Indian Time

Is there really something to that concept many of us have heard about called "Indian Time"? Well, the short version is: yes. In fact, I just returned from a faculty meeting with my colleagues from the Native Studies Department, and one of my Anishnaabe colleagues had a coffee cup which said, "This is the earliest I've ever been late!" We all had a good laugh at that one, because it has such a ring of truth!

I remember my own frustration and confusion when my family and I first moved into the community of Pikogan. Rez dwellers were often invited to attend general meetings at the Great Hall or in the Band Council Office, and there was always an "announcement" (usually by the Anishnaabe police car trolling through the community) telling people that, for example, "We're having a meeting at 1:30. Everybody is invited!" So, of course, my wife and I would wander over to the Great Hall at 1:30 and—guess what? Right! We were the only ones there! In fact, no one had showed up by 2:00 even! But around 2:10 or 2:15, people from the community started wandering in, and

Guess some people just can't handle "Indian Time"!

when the Chief and Band Council finally arrived, the meeting would start—right on time! Of course, not right on *our* time, but everybody in the community was fine with it. No one groused "Where *is* everybody?", or, "Why is the meeting starting so late?" No, nothing like that. In fact, no one *ever* mentioned it. The point is, when everyone was there, the meeting would begin—again, *right on time!*

It's interesting, too, that we quickly became acclimatized to the concept to the point that, within a few weeks, we began showing up at meetings and events "right on time"—meaning a half hour to forty-five minutes later than it had been announced. We were still *usually* the first ones there, but sometimes there were a few people there even *before* us!

Even years later, teaching in the department of Native Studies, the same thing happens. The Coordinator will announce (sometimes days in advance) a faculty meeting, say, for 9:00 a.m. By about 9:30 or 9:45 most of the faculty would be there, but there was one Elder, in particular, who regularly would arrive at least an hour after the announced time. So one time the Coordinator went around to a bunch of the faculty and said, "I'm going to announce that our next faculty meeting will start at 8:30 a.m." Sure enough, she announced it for 8:30 and we all showed up, including the Elder who was typically an hour late, at 9:30—*right on time!*

The concept that Anishnaabe people operate on a different time cycle (commonly referred to, even by Anishnaabe people, as "Indian Time"), attests to a very real cultural difference in attitudes toward what "time" means between Anishnaabe people and most Canadians I know personally. The way I would put it is as follows: it seems that most Anishnaabe people I know tend to resent being rushed or pushed or having to adjust to some kind of "time pressure." When the time is right, it will happen, whatever "it" is: a meeting, a feast, a social gathering, and so on. Scheduling precise appointments, and actually chiding people for being "late" or pressuring them to be there "on time," just isn't part of Anishnaabe reality. I should note that things are changing as the times and contexts change—for example, most of the Anishnaabe professors pretty much show up at class time (well, *most* of the time), but I don't know many Anishnaabe people who seem to be "ruled by the clock" or who even wear wristwatches! (Although there are some exceptions—which only seem to prove the "rule.") To many of my Anishnaabe buddies, it just seems like a foreign concept— kind of unnatural and disrespectful of life's rhythms. I'm not really sure how else to put it, so permit me to provide you with a few more examples, just so you know, and also, I hope, to defuse any frustration you might have about "Indians who are always late!" Let's see what we can do…

Now, I don't want you to get the wrong idea here. Most Anishnaabe people know when they're "late" to a non-Native function or class, or whatever, but it's a new experience for many Anishnaabe people and it's still much more prominent and noticeable in the bush and in the community than in non-Native contexts, such as the urban setting or the university. But the concept is still alive and well and still continues to drive white people nuts! I've tried to figure it out many times (mostly unsuccessfully), but it seems to have something to do with how people lived their lives for thousands of years before the Europeans came along, and it often takes a long time (even 500 years sometimes!) for these values to change. I kind of think of my Anishnaabe buddies as more "process" oriented than "product" oriented, or something along those lines.

I remember being with Normand in the community of Pikogan and I had offered to go with him to pick up his brother in the bush. His brother had gone moose hunting and asked Normand to pick him up in three days "by the bridge" around 50 kilometers down a bush road. Since I was driving, I knew this was going to be a long trip (in that you had to drive about 75 clicks before even *reaching* the bush road!). So here I am, driving at break-neck speed, and Normand finally says something to the effect that I could slow down. It was starting to rain and I was getting tense and I didn't want to drive in the dark, etc., etc. So I said something to the effect that "But if I slow down, we'll be *late!*" Normand, in his wonderful cultural way, said to me, "Shognosh, we're not gonna be late no matter how fast or slow you drive. We'll be right on time." Yeah, right,

I thought... Sure enough, by the time we got there (which I thought was pretty "late"), there was his brother, with his moose already field-dressed when we pulled up. His first words: "Hey, right on time!" I had to laugh because, well, just because it was so funny and so different from my *own* sense of time and, finally, because we got there "right on time!" Yeah, this old Shognosh was starting to catch on!

Wait-time

For non-Anishnaabe teachers in Canada who have Anishnaabe students in their classes, "wait-time" is something else that can be baffling. Wait-time refers to the length of time people in a conversation are willing to wait for a reply after asking a question. When Anishnaabe kids attend non-Anishnaabe schools, for example, the classroom climate seems to be too pressured and teachers don't give enough time for Anishnaabe students to respond after they've been asked a question. I've had quite a few non-Anishnaabe teachers take some of my Anishnaabe Studies courses over the years and I remember asking them about this. The most common response I received from the non-Anishnaabe teachers is they assumed that the Anishnaabe student was either unwilling or unable to answer the question, although they weren't really sure why. As a consequence, Anishnaabe students are often assumed to be "slow" or "uncooperative" when they fail to respond according to non-Anishnaabe cultural standards. What the non-Anishnaabe teacher is usually not aware of are the different timing expectations at work in Anishnaabe interaction. As a teacher with both Anishnaabe and non-Anishnaabe students in my classes, I've noticed that Anishnaabe students like to think about questions posed in class before rushing to answer. It's interesting to see the frustration from both sides. While the non-Anishnaabe students are puzzled by what they consider to be a "slow" response time, the Anishnaabe students comment on how "pushy" non-Anishnaabe people are with language, how they're always in a hurry to hear their own voice and how they like to interrupt people when they're talking.

I remember hearing Ovide Mercredi, the former National Chief of the Assembly of First Nations, speak at the University of Sudbury a few years back. The audience was a mixture of Anishnaabe people and non-Anishnaabe people and when he finished his presentation he invited people to ask questions. After two or three questions a non-Anishnaabe woman stood up and said, "Look, I've noticed that the first few questions have been asked by non-Anishnaabe people. I think we need to give the Indians a chance to ask questions, too!" After a bit of a pause Ovide said very diplomatically to her, "You don't need to worry about the Anishnaabe people here. Just because they're not talking doesn't mean they're not thinking about what is being said. When any of the Anishnaabe people here are ready to ask a question, they will. You don't have to worry about us or feel that you have to stand up for us. We're perfectly capable of doing that for ourselves." Eventually, when the time was right, a number of Anishnaabe people began to ask questions. To me, it goes back to different ways of doing things, different timing expectations and a different perspective on what it means to interact with people in an Anishnaabe kind of way.

Who's Watching the Kids?

One of those commonly shared themes in most Anishnaabe communities is this: don't push your beliefs or ways of thinking and doing things down the throats of others. After I began to catch on to that value, I began to see it at work almost every day in face-to-face interactions in the community where I lived for eleven years. You just didn't see people going around telling other people what to do. The same principle could be seen in how people raised their children in the community. When we first moved to Pikogan, we observed that the kids on the reserve seemed to "run around" with no supervision. From my non-Anishnaabe perspective, the parents seemed to take a "hands-off" approach to child rearing, to say the least! After awhile, though, I began to catch on that the kids in the community were being looked after very carefully.

All of the adults in the community shared a sense of guardianship for the kids. In time, we, too, began to feel more at ease letting our own kids "run free" in the community. We knew that they were being watched by others on the reserve and we began to take on that responsibility, too, when there were kids playing in our "space." From a cultural outsider's perspective, it appeared that the kids were running around "wild". This is no small matter, because it's still often the case that non-Anishnaabe people who are in positions of authority with respect to Aboriginal families and communities (such as the Children's Aid Society), make judgments based on ignorance which have devastating effects on families and communities.

This principle of not forcing your thinking on others accords privacy and freedom of thought and action to another human being—child or adult. Each individual is seen as having a sacred purpose for being. To intrude upon an individual's development and destiny would be rude and inappropriate. As I mentioned above, quite quickly upon entering the community of Pikogan I noticed that far less direct parental control was exerted over children than one sees in my own non-Anishnaabe upbringing. Parents rarely spanked or severely reprimanded their children at Pikogan. Children are disciplined, for sure, but in very subtle ways, ways that are much different than in my own tradition. Children are encouraged to learn by experience and observation. Sometimes this was seen by non-Anishnaabe people living nearby in stereotypical fashion. I've heard non-Anishnaabe people say, for example, "Those Indians just let their kids run wild." And we've all heard (if not used) the expression, "They're acting like a bunch of wild Indians." But it's important to keep in mind that the underlying principle of not forcing one's way of thinking on another is at work here. In the minds of the Anishnaabe people I know personally, each individual is placed on this earth by the Creator to fulfill his or her own destiny. So Anishnaabe parents respect their children's freedom of choice and let their children be as much as possible. After all, in the Anishnaabe view of things, the development of an individual's will to do right is of greater importance than coercing that person to behave in a certain way.

Maintaining Harmony in Face-to-Face Interaction

In many First Nation communities, personal confrontations are avoided whenever possible. Maintaining harmony in one's relationships is the important thing. Among adults, especially, anyone who tries to control or coerce another person to act in a certain way is viewed as "acting like the white man."

One example of this harmony principle can be seen in how people engage in the practices of lending and borrowing in the community. It was really interesting to see the techniques that people in the community used to borrow money, for example. When I first arrived in Pikogan, I was often asked to lend people money. Usually people would say, "I'll pay you back tomorrow." Of course, I took it *literally* and was disappointed when I didn't get paid back the very next day! Eventually I caught on that "tomorrow" meant "sometime in the future." And, you know, I always got paid back. I didn't always get paid back with the money I had lent, but sometimes with gifts of moosemeat or beaver or someone doing me a favour.

Another time, I remember being at a friend's house one day when his cousin, a Band Counselor, came by with a petition to be signed. My friend read the petition and then signed it. Later that day another relative came around with another petition exactly the opposite of the first one. After chatting together for a while my friend then signed the *second* petition. When I saw him sign the second one I thought, "What the hell is he doing? Now he's in big trouble!" When I asked him about it he just shrugged. The important thing in his mind was to maintain the harmony of the relationship at that moment. The fact that he had signed two opposing petitions was no big deal compared to the importance of avoiding tension and maintaining harmony in his kinship relationships.

I remember once I was riding my bike on the rez and one friend who had had a few too many asked to ride it. I said "Sure," and he immediately rode it into the ditch by the side of the road and, well, pretty much wrecked it. I think he was waiting for the "white guy" to get angry (a fun activity for some younger Anishnaabe people to do—"Hey, let's see if we can get some white people pissed off!"—just for fun, y'know?). Anyway, I just smiled and said, "Looks like my bike doesn't work very well." Fortunately, he started laughing instead of pummeling me. Know what I mean? A little consideration and respect can go a long way. Plus, I was able to say it in the language, which helped! And, for what it's worth, his wife, who was watching the whole incident, came out of her house, brought my bike back to her porch and got it up and running again. Seems like some kind of cultural value at work there, although I'm not exactly sure what I would call it. Maybe taking familial responsibility for the (stupid) actions of your spouse? Just guessing...but it *did* help to maintain the harmony of a potentially explosive situation.

Sharing

A corollary to the cultural value of maintaining harmony in all social relations is that of *sharing*. Certainly every culture has some sense that it's good to share things. In fact, before entering the community of Pikogan, I felt that I was a very generous person and one who was quite willing to share. Very quickly, though, I realized that I was really quite a stingy person by the community's standards. It took me a long time to come to the place where I was willing to share freely with those around me, especially my car and my money. Giving gifts, money, possessions and time are an important part of life at Pikogan. Many times I've observed that people who receive such things respond in gratitude and thanksgiving by sharing with those near to them. From my perspective, generosity is rooted in the philosophy that giving furthers the development of relationships. A corollary of this is that by giving to another I am creating a kind of social security net for myself against possible future need. As one person told me, "Sharing things and giving things away keeps our community going."

Non-Interference

As it is with child-raising, the principle of non-interference can be seen operating in everyday interaction in the community. Since most Anishnaabe people are employing this value subconsciously all the time, it is a continuing source of misunderstanding and miscommunication between them and white people. For example, consider how someone informs another person in the community about an upcoming event. Very rarely would the person try to solicit a definite commitment, as often happens in my culture. People relay the information (about an upcoming meeting, for example), but rarely do you hear people saying, "So, will you be there?" or,

"Oh, please come to the meeting!" The person being addressed simply knows she or he is invited to come. No one wants to create a tense moment or disrupt the harmony of a relationship. Nor would you hear the receiver of the news say he or she is not coming. So you can see the kinds of problems that arise when non-Anishnaabe people approach Anishnaabe people on non-Anishnaabe terms and expect them to respond according to the non-Anishnaabe way of doing things. It's such inter-actions—done in ignorance of Anishnaabe ways of life and thinking and ways of doing things—that lead people to say, "Indians are so irresponsible," or, "You can't trust an Indian."

So, where are we?

Again, Anishnaabe social and cultural interactions are the natural outcome of *respect* for others. *Personal confrontations are to be avoided at all costs!* Among Anishnaabe adults, especially, anyone who tries to control other people is viewed as doing something intrinsically "bad" or "white." One of the main complaints that I've heard my friends talk about in relation to non-Anishnaabe people is that, "They're always pushy," "They're always telling you what to do," and "They're always trying to get you to do things their way."

My Wife says that I don't need anymore education...I'm already a "Know-it-all-ogist".

The introduction of western technology into many Anishnaabe communities is changing some of these important cultural values, such as sharing and respect and mutual concern—more often than not for the worse. Before electricity came into many Anishnaabe communities, when somebody killed a moose he would bring the moose back to the village and distribute the meat according to the culturally-proper means of distribution in the community. No family would dare think of hoarding the meat for themselves. What would happen to those without meat? And, how would the meat be preserved anyway? After electricity came into the community one of the first pieces of technology to follow was the freezer. You can imagine what kind of an effect the freezer had on traditional values of sharing. When somebody kills a moose now, he can just throw all the meat in the freezer and it will last all winter. The whole value of sharing meat is changing and, with it, the cultural strength of sharing. It's interesting, too, to think about the term that the Elders in the community coined for that piece of technology in the Anishnaabe language. They call it a "stingy box," because now you don't have to share your meat.

So where does all this leave us? I truly believe that Canadians can learn much about this mysterious thing we call "Life" from Anishnaabe people. And perhaps this journey of learning will help to reduce tension and confrontation in the future. Otherwise, we could all end up in the freezer together…

Would Canada be better off as a Nation if Anishnaabe people would just give up all their traditional ways and languages and live like good Canadians? Obviously I don't think so. Just think about it. A whole new world can open up for you if you're willing to take the time to get to know Anishnaabe people and Anishnaabe ways of thinking and doing things, and that can only make for a stronger, better Canada.

The truth is that most Anishnaabe people already know which non-Anishnaabe ways are worth learning and which ones are not, and they will quickly take advantage of them. But it's generally not a two-way street. In light of the cultural differences Canadians can learn from, perhaps the street should be two-way. When you think about it, whose ways of thinking and doing things, those of Anishnaabe people or non-Anishnaabe people, have more to offer in terms of coping with life in this crazy world? I wonder...

6

So You Think You're Polite?

In my experience living in one Anishnaabe community, I had many opportunities to observe non-Anishnaabe people entering the community in order to "work together" with community members on one project or another. More often than not, the project would be undermined by underlying tension between the Anishnaabe and non-Anishnaabe researchers. I think that one key reason for this is that non-Anishnaabe people, generally speaking, aren't willing to relinquish control of a project. I remember when I worked on a community survey at Pikogan with another non-Anishnaabe. Since I had been involved with the community for a number of years, community members would invariably bring their complaints about other non-

Anishnaabe people working in the community to me, the white guy. It was sometimes awkward to hear Anishnaabe people talking about how white people always want to be the "bosses" of these projects and how they're so "pushy." Suffice it to say, they were usually right. On the other hand, I've had more than a few opportunities to listen to non-Anishnaabe people involved in teaching and research in Anishnaabe communities express frustration about how difficult it is to work with Anishnaabe people, things like: "These people are never on time and they're always laughing at me." (Hmm, I wonder why....) I usually begin any response by saying something along these lines: "In any cross-cultural situation, it's important to learn how to interact appropriately, because what is considered to be rude behavior in one's own culture is often the polite way of behaving in another, and what is considered to be polite behavior in one's own culture is often considered to be very rude in another. So it's important to pay attention to the values underlying these culture-specific ways of doing things."

Sometimes I think it's the small things that foster a climate of confusion, tension and distrust between Anishnaabe people and Canadians. Few who pay any serious attention would disagree that there are different values at work in the everyday lives of Aboriginal people and Canadians. Just watch daily interactions carefully for a while and you begin to see differences in all sorts of things. In this chapter I'll look at some of those small, daily social interactions—the ones that tend to disappear from our radar in our own culture because we sort of *live inside* them. Sort of like how we forget about our shoes unless they start hurting our feet. My point is that these habits of living actually reflect our cultural values, our ways of looking at the world around us—what we consider *reality*. So when our reality starts butting up against another reality—as opposed to steamrolling right over it, which has happened a lot in the relationship of Canada and the First Nations (see the Residential School stuff in chapter three, or the Treaty stuff in chapter twelve)—well hey, it's like when our shoes start hurting—we *notice* it! And it feels uncomfortable. We can feel confused, unsure of ourselves. Embarrassed. And it's usually the small things that cause that reaction initially.

Now, as I've mentioned before, Anishnaabe people seem to be pretty knowledgeable about Canadian ways of thinking and doing things; they've attended Canadian schools, been taught Canadian history and have been forced to live under a different set of rules which govern their everyday lives (the aforementioned Indian Act, which is based exclusively on race). We might say they've been shoehorned into tight, inflexible leather Oxfords and have to keep their soft, pliable moccasins out of sight. (Okay, okay, enough of the shoe metaphor already....) Well, let's turn things around a bit. Given my own experience with Anishnaabe everyday living, I've developed a few calluses from having my cultural toes stepped on (couldn't resist…). I've developed a new perspective on life, broadened my understanding of reality. Maybe I can help you focus your attention appropriately, and so ease the development of your new relationship with First Nations culture in this country. Because we *need* a new relationship! Our primary tendency when we experience cultural vertigo, not unreasonably, is to get out of the situation and avoid it in future. But that's exactly what we *shouldn't* do. We need to acclimatize, acculturate. As we do, the vertigo will fade away—probably not completely, but enough that we can find our way around in this new reality. And remember, I'm your guide, and I *survived*!

Unless we start to pay close attention to the cultural differences and stick with them, rather than hunkering back down inside our own cultural comfort zones, those differences start to add up to the point where Canadians tend to think, as many have mentioned to me over the years, that Native people are peculiar, almost weird, in the different ways they think and do things. And that gets to the heart of this survival guide. If we can focus on some of those subtle differences and draw out the values that underlie them, then we can begin to make real progress in building bridges of understanding between Anishnaabe people and Canadians, and really start to make the relationship a two-way street. Okay, here we go!

Eye Contact

Let's start with an easy one that I bet most of you have heard about in some form or another. It goes something like this: always avoid direct eye contact when talking with Native people. Or, put another way, Native people don't like non-Natives to maintain sustained eye contact when they're interacting. Ever heard that before? Is it true? Well, in my experience, I would say, "Yes and no." It is true that direct and sustained eye contact when talking with Native people can be considered very intrusive, even rude. But that's not to say, "Hey, never look directly in the eyes of Indians when you're talking to 'em!" Kind of like they're vampires or something! The point is, as it is with many differing cultural values, the meaning here is quite subtle. (Okay, so eye contact isn't an "easy" one after

Remember now...no eye contact!...
First they take yer blood... then yer land!

all.) I've been hanging out with Anishnaabe people for almost thirty years and it's pretty rare that I don't maintain pretty steady eye contact when we're talking together. There are times, though, when I would never maintain direct or sustained eye contact, such as when an Elder is giving a teaching, or someone is talking about something very personal. I noticed it regularly in the community of Pikogan.

For example, one evening I was visiting with a family and there were maybe 15 people gathered around the kitchen area and the kitchen table, just talking and joking and having a good time. At one point, though, and I forget exactly how it got started, one of the Elders sitting at the kitchen table started to tell a story, obviously a serious one rather than an entertaining one, and you could see virtually everyone (except for the small children, maybe), lower their eyes as the Elder started telling the story—which really was a traditional teaching in the form of a story. In that kind of context, even Native people themselves won't maintain direct eye contact with the speaker, out of respect, mostly, but also to let the speaker know they are taking his words seriously.

But such a value seems to get non-Natives confused. When they hear about it from a friend or in a Native Studies class, they're not sure what's going on. Over the years I've had dozens of non-Natives, who were really interested in learning about Anishnaabe ways of thinking and doing things, ask me, "What should I do when I'm talking with a Native person? You seem to be teaching us that we should always look down and never make eye contact because Native people think it's rude." Whoa! Hold on a minute! There *is* a challenge here. Since the interaction is subtle and nuanced, the tendency when explaining it is to oversimplify, and then the oversimplification risks reinforcing stereotypes rather than clarifying them. My response is usually something like this: "Oh, no, I didn't mean to imply that you should never look a Native person in the eye when you're talking together! In fact, in my own experience, there's plenty of eye contact, and laughter, and all sorts of little things going on when you're in a conversation." But then I continue: "But there are times when we non-Natives do tend to stare at people while talking with them, and I've heard tons of Native people talk about how they feel that their personal space is being invaded when non-Natives stare at them and maintain sustained eye contact. The important thing to remember is that there is a different value at work here, and it gets quite subtle. You've got to pay attention, watch carefully, and have respect for the situation—even when it seems as mundane as eye contact. Sure, we all look people in the eye when we're talking with them, but don't overdo it!" I mean, nobody likes space invaders, right? Well, interacting with Anishnaabe people really brings that truth home. See how much distance we've already covered with this small thing about eye contact?

Forms of Address

My two oldest daughters grew up attending a band-run school in the First Nation community of Pikogan. It was an experience I'm sure they'll never forget and one that has given them a bicultural outlook on life. When we moved to Sudbury in 1990 after spending eleven years in the community of Pikogan, all three of my daughters began attending a non-Anishnaabe school for the first time in their lives. We wondered how they would adjust and, believe me, it was tough for them at first. It wasn't just the language difference, it was something deeper. The first thing I remember them having to adjust to was what to call their teachers and others in positions of authority. At Pikogan, everyone in the community is on a first-name or nick-name basis: Elders, parents, the chief, children, dogs—everyone. And, of course, all the teachers in the community school are called by their first names by the students. In most non-Anishnaabe schools, though, the policy is to call teachers and other school officials by their formal titles or "Mr." and "Mrs." For our kids, learning to call their teachers "Mr. or Mrs. So-and-so" was quite different and often quite confusing. After all, when you've gone to a school where you call all your teachers by their first names, it takes some time to learn that calling teachers by their first names is just not acceptable in most non-Anishnaabe schools!

So You Think You're Polite?

Doing "Introductions"

I remember my first experiences with something as simple as "meeting someone" or doing "introductions." In my tradition I was always taught, when first meeting someone, especially another man, to give him a firm, "manly" (whatever the hell *that's* supposed to mean!) handshake, look him right in the eye and say something like, "Hi, I'm Roger Spielmann, and you?" When I first tried that at Pikogan, I could tell pretty quickly that something was quite different in the way one does "introductions." The first time I went up to an Elder I stuck out my hand, ready for the "manly" handshake, and nothing happened for a few seconds. Now, think about it. A "few seconds" can seem like a looong time in that kind of situation! Eventually, the Elder stuck out two fingers and limply pulled on my fingers! "What a wimpy handshake," I thought! A few seconds later he said, "I know you, Shognosh."

Now, I had never met the Elder before in my life, but that leads us into another subtle aspect of "doing introductions" in the community. It's like, when do you "know somebody"? In my culture, you can say you "know somebody" after you've met the person in some formal or informal setting. But the way people get to "know" someone in the community of Pikogan is not by going up and introducing themselves, but by asking someone *else* in the community something like, "Who's that guy?" If the person happens to have heard your name or seen you around, then he'll tell the person who asked him, "Oh, that's Shognosh." *Now* he "knows" me and there's no need for doing a non-Native handshake or "introducing yourself." You know each other.

Of course, I was surprised a number of times when we first moved into the community that everyone seemed to *know* me while I hardly knew anyone! Ah, then I started catching on by both observing what people do when "someone new" comes visiting the reserve and by asking my (up to that point) one friend about it. Thank God for cultural friends! He told me, basically, how it worked in the community and quite quickly I found myself doing the same thing. Instead of "introducing" myself to someone I didn't know, I would just ask someone else if they knew the person. They usually did and would tell me his (or her) name, at which point I "knew" them and never had to introduce myself. They had likely done the same thing to find out who *I* was, so we both *knew* each other even though we had never met! Works like a charm!

But when the occasional non-Native would come around doing the non-Native "introduction" thing, they often went away perplexed about how "rude" these Indians were—they really didn't want to shake your hand or tell you their name! How rude. But, of course, my Anishnaabe buds were actually doing the "polite" and culturally relevant way of "getting to know someone" or "introducing themselves." It was just different. And, for whatever reason, *I* would often have the non-Natives coming up to me, I guess because they must have thought that I had it all figured out, and *I* would end up being the one telling them how to do things in a culturally appropriate way. The white guy teaching other white guys how to act appropriately in a Native community! Just didn't seem right, but I *did* want them to learn that the people weren't being "rude"; the non-Natives were just expecting them to play by their rules and, when they didn't, they figured the people were rude! And this kind of scenario continues to play itself out almost every day at the university; non-Natives asking *me* (why don't they ask the Anishnaabe professors?) how to do things in an Anishnaabe appropriate way! See? Something small can lead to huge misunderstandings, increased tension and reinforced stereotypes.

Making Direct and Indirect Requests

I remember an experience I had shortly after entering the Anishnaabe community, which began to clue me in to some of the basic cultural differences existing between Anishnaabe people and Canadians. I was new to the community and just beginning to learn to speak the Anishnaabe language. One day my car broke down and I had it towed to the nearby town to have it repaired. Not wanting to stay at the garage all day, I decided to call one of my friends from the reserve, an Elder who was teaching me his language and his way of life. I got him on the phone and asked, in what I thought was a polite way of making a request, *"Gigaagii biinda naajiwiizhinan naa?"* [Could you come and pick me up?] He hesitated and then said, *"Ehe"* [Yes]. When he arrived, I jumped into his truck. He turned to me and, as only a friend could, said, "Don't say, *'Gigaagii biinda naajiwiizhinan naa?'*, just say, *'Biindaa naajiwishin!'"* [Come and get me!]. Here I was trying to be polite by using the kind of polite asking technique that I learned in my culture: putting the request in the form of a question, to give him the opportunity to say no, he couldn't come. But to his ears, the way I asked him was rude. It was as if I was questioning his ability to drive or something. The funny thing is that his way of asking for a favour sounded rude to my ears! The difference is that in Anishnaabe culture cooperation is assumed, whereas in my non-Anishnaabe cultural way of doing things, people seem more comfortable when cooperation is negotiated.

So, now you're thinking, "It may seem weird, but if I turn my politeness into my rudeness, then I'm practicing *their* politeness. Cool. Got it." Ah…no. Too bad it isn't that simple. Actually, in Anishnaabe interaction the strategy of being *indirect* is really the conventionally *polite* way of making requests for favours. Because in almost thirty years I've never heard an Anishnaabe person say "no" to a request. I'll repeat that: in almost thirty years I've never heard an Anishnaabe person say "no" to a request. Of course, while cooperation is assumed, Anishnaabe people are savvy enough to know that often there are other reasons why a person may not be able to cooperate. But it's impolite to make that person have to say no. The value of *maintaining the harmony of the moment* is just too strong in most Anishnaabe communities for one person to actually say "no" to another person. So over the years Anishnaabe people have developed this nifty way of asking for things without ever putting themselves in the position of potentially forcing the other person to say "no" to them! And they also know the situations where someone just won't *say* no, and where it's therefore more polite to be direct, as in my scenario above. Geddit? Either way, direct or indirect, no one gets hurt feelings, no one goes away mad. It's just the way it's done. Pretty smart, those Anishnaabe, sez I.

Check out the following conversational example where someone requesting a favour uses a conventionally *indirect* strategy which the Shognosh (white guy; me) doesn't catch on to. This episode sticks with me because it went so much against the grain of acceptable conversational interaction in my own culture. We first moved into the community of Pikogan in the summer of 1979. The use of the Anishnaabe language was, and is, extremely strong in the community and the Elders were patient and kind as they taught me how to speak their language.

Interestingly, though, the Elders and other community members somehow figured that when I was becoming conversationally fluent in the language that I also must know how to *use* the language appropriately in conversational interaction. In our second year in the community, when I had reached a certain degree of conversational fluency, I remember receiving a telephone call from one of the guys with whom I had become friends. After some small talk, the conversation went like this:

Him: *Anezhitaayan maanigiizhigag e onaagoshig?*
      [What are you doing Saturday night?]
Me: *Gaa gegoon.*
      [Nothing]
              [5 second pause]
Him: *Maanoj*
      [Never mind.] [hangs up the phone]

I was quite puzzled by this interaction the first time it happened. At the time, using my non-Anishnaabe intuition, I assumed that his question was a *pre-invitation* utterance, so I "heard" that utterance as one that was doing the work of finding out if my wife and I were available to do something with the caller and his wife on Saturday night. As is common in my culture, a "pre-invitation" utterance is often used to find out about one's availability before the actual invitation is offered.

Thus, I expected the next utterance to be something along the lines of: "So do you guys want to come over for dinner on Saturday?" Instead, where I was expecting the "actual" invitation to occur, he hung up. If the whole thing had stopped there, I might not have caught on to what was happening, at least not at this particular time. As it turned out, however, he called back two more times that day and the conversation proceeded in exactly the same manner! By the third time, after he had hung up again, I was beginning to get quite irritated. I remember saying to my wife, "What the hell is going on? He keeps calling to ask what we're doing Saturday night and when I tell him that we don't have any plans he hangs up!"

Then he called again. The conversation followed exactly the same pattern, except this time, instead of hanging up, he quietly asked, *"Gigaagii gaanawenimawaag naa nidabinojizhimag Maanigiizhigag e onaagoshig?"* [Can you guys baby-sit for us on Saturday night?]. I assured him that it was no problem and we'd be glad to baby-sit for them. Then it hit me. Because I wasn't "tuned in" to appropriate ways of doing things in the community, such as the appropriate way of making a request for a favour, I had forced him to play the "game" by *my* cultural rules—to ask me directly for a favour in a situation where the opening was there for me to say *no*. From his perspective he was taking a real social risk. What if I had had to say no? We'd both have been embarrassed. The harmony would have been upset. Once I got this awakening (a rude one from the Anishnaabe perspective), I suddenly saw the phenomenon all around me on a daily basis—people making requests *without ever actually asking for anything!*

Saying Goodbye

So, many interactions between Anishnaabe people and non-Anishnaabe people get off to a bad start simply because most non-Anishnaabe people are not aware of how to "be polite" from an Anishnaabe perspective. Consider saying "good-bye" to each other. In non-Anishnaabe interaction, for example, it's assumed that a certain formula will be followed when people are done talking with each other, something like:

A: Well, I better get going.
B: Yeah, me, too. See you later.
A: Okay, seeya.

In the community of Pikogan, as in many First Nations communities, however, "saying goodbye" is done, more often than not, by simply turning and walking away when one is finished speaking. Now, certainly this would be considered very rude to many Canadians, but it's a polite way of "saying good-bye" in many Anishnaabe communities. The same holds true for telephone conversations. I remember talking with one of the Elders on the telephone and all of a sudden he hung up. At first I thought that I must have said something to offend him. As this pattern kept repeating itself, though, I began to realize that I was the one expecting some kind of formulaic leave-taking at the end of the conversation. For my Anishnaabe friends, however, when the conversation is over, they hang up. What need is there to say more?

Not Contradicting

Anishnaabe people will do just about anything to avoid contradicting each other, at least in public. And that practice—like the indirect requests dealt with above—illustrates perfectly what I talked about in the last chapter: the importance of maintaining harmony in all social situations, whenever possible. Now, I'm not saying that Canadians don't try to do these things as well, but they're done differently among Anishnaabe people. I think the underlying value at play in non-contradiction is that each individual has the right to have and express his or her own opinion. It seems the "polite" thing is basically to agree with whatever someone says, even if the "agreement" is really non-committal—it's a way of avoiding confrontation even if you think that what the person is expressing is bullshit. Everyone goes away happy, and then you can gossip to your heart's content when you hang out at home or with your other buddies.

Now, you might be thinking, "Hey, lots of Canadians play that social game too. We've all heard from our mothers what Thumper's mother said in *Bambi*: 'If you can't say something nice, don't say anything at all.'" Right, you got it from *Bambi*! A sentimental Disney cartoon! Right up there with *Pocahontas*! I'll grant that Canadians know the value of non-contradiction, but in practice they see it as sentimental. The more serious value is to challenge the opinion you disagree with—shoot it down. Isn't that what you're taught in high school and university? Argue your point, challenge superficial thinking, call a spade a spade?

Well in Anishnaabe World non-contradiction isn't sentimental. If everyone in the community is playing by the same cultural rules, rules which have been used for thousands of years, then it doesn't seem so wacky. In fact, a common approach when one senses that an open confrontation *might* erupt is to give the pretense of agreement, and if you can't bring yourself to do that, then leave the situation—walk away from it. And, when you think about it, it's a fact that these people survived intact as nations for thousands of years before the arrival of the Europeans, and the very fact that they've survived so long without our help only solidifies the fact that the ways they've developed of interacting over the years without killing each other off really do *work*.

So You Think You're Polite?

It's All Right There in the Language

When I began teaching in the Department of Native Studies at the University of Sudbury, I noticed an interactional phenomenon which, in retrospect, I remember having encountered many times over the years spent hanging out with Anishnaabe (Ojibwe and Algonquin) people. I was talking with one of my students at the time and I happened to ask him about one of his assignments that was due.

> Me: "Did you finish your essay yet?"
> Him: "Yeah."
> Me: "Oh, good. Did you turn it in?"
> Him: "Well, I'll have it finished by Tuesday."

I couldn't help having some fun with him, nor could I stop myself from trying to figure out what the heck was going on with that particular conversation. My initial thinking went something like this: the real answer to my question was "No." So, really, his "yes" meant "no." But what did *that* mean? Being a close friend as well as his prof, I asked him about his response and we began to get a bit deeper into what was going on in his Anishnaabe mind by analyzing it a bit. The best place to start, I figured, would be with his own explanation of the interaction; in other words, how does *he* explain it? He thought about it for a minute, then offered this explanation: "I guess I was thinking that I'm *almost* finished with the essay in the sense you were asking about, so in my mind it IS finished." What he's pointing to here, I believe, is that, in the Anishnaabe way of thinking, the boundaries between "past" and "present," "finished" and "ongoing," "product" and "process," are much different than in my own non-Anishnaabe way of thinking. On the other hand, he may have merely been trying to get off the hook for having been caught! But I doubt it. I've observed so many similar kinds of interaction, usually between Anishnaabe people themselves, that I'm inclined to accept his explanation as reflecting a quite different way of thinking and relating to other people.

For example, consider the following interaction:

Rob: "Yeah, I quit smoking."
Me: "Oh, yeah? When?"
Rob: "Well, I haven't really quit yet, but I'm thinking about it."

I was standing around having a smoke outside the university with some of the Anishnaabe students when Rob came up, chatted a bit, and then told me that he had quit smoking. Of course, as we were talking he pulled out a pack of cigarettes and lit one up! Everyone laughed along with him, but part of the humour of the situation had to do, I believe, with the distinctly Anishnaabe thinking in relation to "process" and "product," "ongoing" and "finished."

Another time, three of us, me and two Anishnaabe buddies, were driving down the road and I asked one of my buddies if he stayed in touch with John, who had moved away a few years earlier. He had been close friends with John.

Me: "Do you still stay in touch with John?"
Him: "Oh, for sure. Well, I haven't spoken to him since he left, but…"

Again, much laughter ensued! As we were all friends (and academics, for better or for worse), we engaged in some mini-analysis of how he had responded. His explanation was, "Well, I guess I answered like that because in my mind John will always be my friend, whether or not I ever see him or talk to him again."

In his book *Dancing With A Ghost* (1996), Rupert Ross offers support for this Anishnaabe-specific difference in thinking and categorizing between Anishnaabe people and non-Anishnaabe Canadians, a difference reflected in the very structure of Algonquian languages. He writes:

Aboriginal people have regularly spoken to me about their verb-based languages. They describe their "verb-world" as one where each person's primary focus is not on each separate thing but on all the movements and relationships *between* things. The verb focus is on the many processes in which we all participate, at every instant in every day. (54)

Ross's comment just reinforces what I've been saying throughout this chapter: these everyday interactions tell us something of how Anishnaabe ways of thinking and doing things can be so very different from the way most Canadians think and view the world around them. But if we're willing to really pay attention—really *listen*—we can learn a lot about a different way of thinking and viewing the world that can enlarge our reality, as well as go a long way to defusing the tension, misunderstanding and stereotypes that persist in compromising the relationship between Canada and the First Nations.

So, are you being polite or being rude?

7

How To Learn Anishnaabe
In Two Weeks Or Less!…

In this chapter I want to pick up on Rupert Ross's comment at the end of the last chapter, that many cultural differences are embedded in the very language of the Anishnaabe. I'll try to answer some of the basic questions I've heard over the years from both Native people and non-Native Canadians about Native languages. Revitalizing the Native language is a burning concern in most First Nation communities. That's why I decided to dedicate this chapter to the issue of language and how important it is for Native people trying to retain their culture and identity. What I really want to do is show you how the values I've been talking about in the last two chapters are right there in the grammar and syntax. Wait! Hold on! I can make it fun! *Trust* me… And because the life of the language is so crucial to Anishnaabe people, parts of this chapter are aimed more directly at my Anishnaabe buddies, but you Canadian readers are invited to listen in and try to grasp what Anishnaabe people are up against when it comes to learning their languages and keeping them alive.

So, anyway, here's the first question.

How difficult is it to learn to speak a Native language?

I can tell you from personal experience that learning to speak a Native language such as Ojibwe or Cree is pretty damn near impossible. Each has more than a million words and particles and morphemes and stuff that linguists call by names that they must have gotten by reading science fiction books. Like, I'm not sure if there are really a million of those kinds of things, but it seems like it. So the most important thing to remember about trying to learn a Native language is this: Forget it.

Okay, so I'm half-joking. The deal is that the Anishnaabe language (from here on referred to as *Anishnaabemowin*), like most Native languages in Canada, is such a difficult language to learn that you either have to make a lifetime commitment to it or you're never gonna speak it well, if at all.

How to Learn Anishnaabe

I remember when I was first learning the Anishnaabe language in the community of Pikogan. I was with a group of Elders outside at the reserve watching some young kids play hockey in the middle of the winter. It was like thirty below and we were freezing. Well, I was freezing, anyway. After awhile one of the Elders turns to me and politely asks, "*Giigaawajinan naa?*", which means, "Are you cold?" Now, I wanted to answer her with a kind of funny response I had learned recently from another Elder, which was, "*Ehe, nigichii-mashkaawidye*", which means, "Yes, I'm freezing my ass off!" But I kind of forgot the exact phrase and what came out of my mouth was, "*Ehe, nigichii-minokwidiye*", which means, "Yes, I have a really nice ass." Well, the Elder immediately went into fits of laughter and turned to her friends and said, "I asked the white guy if he was cold and he says he has a real nice ass!" See what I mean? It can be pretty tough trying to learn all of the intricacies of a Native language in order to speak it properly. By the way, Elders at Pikogan still remind me of that incident years later... ("*Oh, Shognosh, kigichii-minokwidiye!*").

So, the deal is this: whether you're Anishnaabe or not, if you make a commitment to learn to speak an Aboriginal language, you're gonna have two strikes against you from the very start. Just don't give up!

Next question, please.

Tell us a bit about the Anishnaabe language.

First you have to figure out what a "question" is... But seriously, Anishnaabemowin belongs to the great Algonquian family of languages in North America. Other Algonquian languages include Cree, Algonquin, Montagnais, Attikamekh, Blackfoot, and Micmac, to name but a few. Like many North American Indian languages, Anishnaabemowin has a very rich set of prefixes and suffixes that can be attached to words to indicate such things as subjects and objects of verbs, tenses, whether or not the speaker knows that the events being reported are facts, whether a statement is positive or negative, etc. See what I mean about how complex it gets? To a speaker of English, the hundreds and even thousands of different forms of the Anishnaabe verb can be quite challenging to learn, or, as I said earlier, pretty damn near impossible.

What are some of the differences between English and Anishnaabe?

One should keep in mind that language differences really reflect differences in ways of thinking and looking at the world around us, and this is one of the areas that seems to cause much confusion and misunderstanding between Native people and those of the non-Native variety.

For example, Anishnaabemowin is, in a very real sense, a non-sexist language. By that I mean that there is no specification of gender in the language itself. The third person pronoun, *wiin*, does not specify whether a male or a female is being referred to. That can only be determined by context. So it's pretty damn confusing for someone who speaks Anishnaabe as a mother tongue to speak English. The Native language is pretty much all the Elders speak in many of the northern First Nation communities, so when they do try to speak English things like "he" and "she" are pretty much thrown into any sentence at random, such as: "My daughter, he's getting married on Saturday," or, "My son, she's real ugly." But it seems to suggest that there was a much more egalitarian relationship between men and women in Anishnaabe culture than in European cultures. I mean, there it is, built right into the language itself. Pretty nifty, don't you think?

Another interesting feature of Anishnaabe which is distinct from English is that Anishnaabe has what is referred to as a *hierarchy of person*, which reflects the very basic cultural value of *respect*. In the language, the second person, "you," always takes grammatical priority. You can say *Niwaabamaa*, which means, "I see him (or her)" but the construction for "I see you," *giiwaabamin*, puts the "you" pronoun at the beginning of the construction and relegates the first person to the end of the word. So the second person always comes first in the language, which reflects a very strong cultural preference of considering others, be they individuals, family or community, as more important than self.

Also, something which sometimes surprises non-Natives is that there is no word for "please" or "apologize" in Anishnaabemowin. This can lead non-Natives to make assumptions about Native people which just aren't true. For example, a statement which we have heard on more than one occasion is: "Indians are so rude, they never say 'please'." That is not to say, however, that there are not culture-specific ways of being polite or of repairing broken friendships. But those ways of doing things are different between cultures, which often tends to lead to cross-cultural misunderstandings and reinforcing stereotypes.

Another major distinction between English and Anishnaabemowin, and again related to different ways of thinking and viewing the world, is in the verb morphology. The verb is the heart of the Anishnaabe language and the verb morphology, or how a verb is "put together" in the language, is extremely complex. There are, in fact, four different kinds or categories of verbs in Anishnaabe—based on whether the subject or object is animate (that is, considered to be a living entity in the culture) or inanimate (that is, considered to be in some sense non-living) and whether the construction of the sentence is transitive (where there is a subject and an object) or intransitive (where there is a subject only). Now, the distinction between what is animate and what is inanimate is not always clear to the non-speaker and relates to a distinctly Anishnaabe way of perceiving the world. In most dialects of the Anishnaabe language, for example, a "rock" is considered to be animate or a living entity—which relates to a traditional Anishnaabe view of person-objects which are other than human but which have the same ontological status—that is, the same qualities as beings. Whew! Gettin' pretty heavy. You grammar phobes are starting to twitch I bet. Sorry! I'll lighten it up, right now!

Some bridge-building survival phrases:

Aanii!   *Aanishnaa?*
(ah-**NEE**)!   (**AH**-nee-**SHNAA**)?
Hi!   How's it going?

       Nishin.   *Giin dash?*
       (nish-**IN**)   (**GEEN** dush)?
       Fine.   How About you?

Aabishenjibayan?
(ah-beesh-**ENJ**-ibaayin)?
Where do you come from?

       Wikwemikong   *ndoonjibaa*
                          (**NDOONJ**-ibaa)
       (name of place)   I come from...

Gaa waabaamin!
(gaa-**WAA**-baa-min)
See ya!

Try it! They'll love it! And don't worry if they laugh. Anishnaabe *love* to laugh! Especially at White people!...

You Already Speak Anishnaabe (You just don't know it yet)

Okay, this section is primarily for the Anishnaabe people reading this book, so I don't want you non-Native types to get confused here. Just listen and learn for a few minutes. Kind of like the title of the book by Vine Deloria called, *We Talk, You Listen.* And, hey, this may provide you with a great opportunity to start learning some of the Anishnaabe language yourself! People take it as a sign of respect and friendship if they see you making an effort to learn their idiom. And that can be really important when your car breaks down at night on the highway through the rez and you've forgotten to charge your cell phone.

I didn't think they could turn any whiter!

How to Learn Anishnaabe

Here's a little dialogue:

Some Anishnaabe person:
>*Giidanishnaabemon naa?*
>(Do you speak your language?)

Your answer: Not really.

Sound like you? Somebody asks you if you speak your Aboriginal language and you tell 'em, "Not really?" If you answer "yes," then this section is gonna be perfect for you. Well, not perfect, maybe, but it's gonna help you realize that you already speak your Aboriginal language, *you just don't know it yet!* Now, let's start with a little quiz. Do you hear your Native language being spoken in your home? No? Then it's strike one against you. But, hey, no big deal. Like, at least you speak one language, right? But because you're an Anishnaabe and you don't speak your Native language very well, you are terrified to even try speaking it. In fact, you might even think that you can't speak it. I remember one of my Anishnaabe buddies telling me once that, "My mouth is designed in such a way that it is impossible to properly pronounce an Anishnaabe word." Needless to say, I just let it go at that… The point is that your inability to speak your Native language has made you believe that you can't speak it at all. Wrong. See, like, I have a secret for you: *you already speak your native language!* You just don't know it yet.

So don't worry. Remember our little secret (although I suppose it's no longer a secret anymore now that I've put it *in this book*): So, okay, the secret is out: You already know how to speak your Native language. You just don't *know* that you know. And the reason you don't know that you know is because it's locked up there somewhere in your Anishnaabe heads. So here's the good news. This section is going to get you started on the road to conversational fluency in your language by introducing our new, revolutionary method of language learning. It's called "The Full Air Method"!

Here's how it works: fill the air with all the words you know in your Native language. As long as you're using whatever you already know, there's a good chance another speaker of the language is going to try to understand what you're saying. He or she might even actually understand something you say without much trouble. That'd be neat, eh?

Now, let's face it, you all know some words in your Native language, even if you never let them slip out of your mouth. In Anishnaabemowin, for example, you probably know, or at least have *heard*, words like *"Biizhaan maampii!"* (Come here!), or *"Niiwi-wiisin"* (I'm hungry). Now, using our basic rule (fill the air with words you know) there's really no reason ever to say "Come here!" or, "I'm hungry" again in English. Ever. Even when you're talking to someone who only speaks English, just use *"Biizhaan maampii"* and *"Niiwi wiisin"* all the time. If they don't speak your language, don't worry. They'll catch on eventually. And if they don't, who cares? You'll be dazzling them with what they think is an extensive knowledge of your Native language. That's right, fool 'em. The important thing is that you're speaking your language!

So remember: don't be shy to use your Native language when talking with non-Native people. Like, it's your land they live on, right? And they forced you to learn *their* language. So it's about time that you put a little pressure on them to get on the stick and realize that your Native language is every bit as good as their language.

And hey, you Canadian readers who just got let in on my little secret. Just remember what I've been telling you: "A little language goes a long way." Why not start yelling *"Biizhaan maampi?"* to your spouse or kids when you need them? They might find it cool! You might start a trend! Who *knows* where it could lead? Wow, I'm getting goosebumps just thinkin' of it...

Okay, Anishnaabe types, first thing. Remember all that stuff about masculine and feminine in English? Well, forget it. I've got some good news for you. There *is* no masculine or feminine in your language, at least if you speak a language in the Algonquian language family. That's good news! The not so good news is that you've got animate (living) and inanimate (non-living). Let's stick with the good news, eh? So, the rule when talking about "him" or "her" is to just use *"wiin."* That can be either "him" or "her" in Anishnaabemowin. Simple, huh? So if you wanna find out who someone is, just ask *"Awenen dash wiin?"* ("Who's that guy?" or, "Who's that chick?"). Works the same whether you're asking about a guy or a girl. No muss, no fuss. You can't miss.

So let's have a little mini-lesson here. You know *"wiin,"* right? How about *"niin"* (me), *"giin"* (you), *"wiinawa"* (them), and *"giinawa"* (youse). So now you never have to answer someone in English when they ask, "Who's coming with me?" Just say *"niin"* (me). Use it whenever you can.

Now for some simple phrases in the past tense. It's easy. Just take any verb. You already know *"biizhaa"* (he/she is coming) and *"maajaa"* (he/she is leaving), right? So just add *"ni"* (short for *"niin"*), then add *"gii"* (past tense) and put it together in front of the verb *"maajaa."* Presto! *"Nigii maajaa"* (I left). Or take *"wiisin"* and do the same thing *"Nigii wiisin"* (I ate). Easy! Remember, though, every dialect is slightly different, so what works in one dialect may not work in another one. But the Elders are smart and they'll be able to tell the difference. So don't worry about it!

A common word that I often heard in the village of Pikogan was *"Aadidook,"* which means, "I don't know." Now, the phrase "I don't know" can mean a lot of different things. Sometimes it's simply a profession of ignorance about what has been asked. At other times it can mean, "I know what you're asking, but I don't want to deal with it right now." Or, it can mean, "It's none of your business." As I told you in chapter six, people who ask direct questions are often seen as being very *rude* in the community where I lived, especially non-Natives who suggested doing things the way a non-Native would. I would often hear people use this phrase as an alternative to saying "no" to a request. I remember one time being at a friend's house at Pikogan when a relative came over and asked my friend, "Does your wife have any money?" Instead of answering "yes" or "no" (after all, he might not, in fact, have known), or going to ask his wife directly if she had any money, he answered *Aadidook* ("I don't know."). The person who came to borrow money knew how to play by the cultural rules and responded with *Maanoj* ("Never mind."), and let the matter drop.

So here's the deal in a nutshell. As I mentioned earlier, there is perhaps no more important, burning issue in any Aboriginal community in Canada than to *keep the Aboriginal language strong* in each First Nation. Language is the soul of a people and many Elders, from a variety of First Nations traditions, maintain that a nation which respects itself speaks, preserves, cultivates and develops its language. Some Elders go so far as to say that, if one doesn't speak his/her Aboriginal language, that person lacks a deeply-rooted sense of identity and is "not fully Anishnaabe."

Many living in Canada never give much thought to what it is about language that evokes such strong feelings in people.

You speak a language and it never crosses your mind that your language might die. But what if your kids were forced to learn another language in order to become educated? What if you, as a parent or grandparent, were no longer able to communicate with your own children or grandchildren because you no longer shared a common language? Or what if you were beaten for speaking your mother tongue? What if people ridiculed your language as primitive and deficient? What if you were told that you could no longer speak your mother tongue? What if you were forbidden from using your language to pray or worship God or teach your kids your values? All of this happened to generations of First Nations people in Canada.

I want to close this discussion by returning to my initial question: why is it important to support the renewal and preservation of Aboriginal languages? First, the studying, preserving and teaching of Aboriginal languages is a personal and powerful statement of respect. Further, understanding the importance of Aboriginal languages to First Nations people, and the reasons for revitalizing and preserving them as languages used in everyday interaction, provides non-Native people in Canada with some resources for exploring and understanding *alternative* ways of thinking, behaving and perceiving the world around us. Monocultural perspectives in today's world can be dangerous in that they encourage only one way of thinking and looking at the world. Further, Aboriginal languages are important keys to the survival of distinct and thriving cultures and world views. Could it be that Aboriginal languages can provide Canadians with solutions to individual and social problems? Perhaps these languages can teach us different ways of thinking about justice, the environment, human relations, spirituality, and resource management. As we've already seen, the Anishnaabe language can teach us much about basic human values such as generosity, honesty, relationships and physical/ emotional needs. In *First Nations Family Justice* (Awasis Agency of Northern Manitoba, 1997), George Muswagon writes:

> Language is the medium through which history, culture and world view are transmitted; therefore the best connection to historical roots are First Nations languages... It is their particular way of viewing the world, and their place in it, that sets First Nations people apart from non-First Nations people. This world view has never really been lost; it remains intact in the languages. (40)

There is reason to be optimistic. First Nations across North America are working hard to reverse the erosion of languages by defining and implementing culturally appropriate curricula and teaching methods to combat this loss. But the battle is far from over; I trust that this brief discussion will help you grasp a sense of the importance and urgency of preserving and revitalizing Aboriginal languages today as the foundation for preserving and strengthening Aboriginal nationhood and identity.

So, to come back to where we started (hey, full circle again! Cool!): how hard is it to learn an Aboriginal language? It's pretty damn hard, but you can do it if you put your mind to it. So, like the Nike commercial says, "Just Do It!"

8

Traditional Education: Sometimes We're "Teachers" and Sometimes We're "Students"

A key component of what is commonly referred to as "traditional education" shared by virtually all First Nations people is that the unknown is made accessible by its connection to the known. The principle here is that learning happens not only when one *understands* the relationship of new ideas to what is already known and understood. We often *know* stuff before we're even aware that we do—for Anishnaabe people there is a deep linkage of the known to the unknown. For example, the kind of knowledge required to make such decisions as where to move one's camp or where to go to hunt for moose, was and is commonly accessed through dreams, visions, spirit visitors, ceremonies, and so on, rather than through books or theories as in the western tradition. I remember an experience I had sitting with Okinawe and Wini (**Win**-nee) on Okinawe's porch one evening. We were just talking about life and, out of the blue, Wini turned to me, pointed at Okinawe, and said (in his language), "You know, Okinawe used to be able to fly." He said it very matter-of-factly, but it almost knocked me over! Okinawe used to be able to fly? Human beings flying just isn't part of my experience, I'm sad to say! When I timidly asked Wini to tell me more, he said, "Before the white man came, the Creator gave the gift of flight to Okinawe so that he could travel vast distances very quickly. Then he would come back and tell the community where there was a moose, or where the beavers had made their house, especially during times when we didn't have enough to eat." Again, Wini said it as if it was the most natural thing in the world, but it blew my mind! I knew Pikogan had not been established until the 1950s, but until now it had never really dawned on me that Okinawe had lived over half his life in a *pre-contact* world. Yet, after I began hearing similar stories over the years while living at Pikogan, it started to make sense to me. Surely the Creator wasn't going to let His people go hungry, and He chose Okinawe to be the "scout" for the rest of the community. Just because it didn't fit my western view of reality didn't mean it wasn't true. And I believe it *is* true. When I further questioned Wini if Okinawe could still fly, he responded, "Oh, there's no need for him to fly anymore.

Now we have grocery stores." Now, my western mind (like those of my Canadian readers I'll lay odds) was boggled by this. I mean, *how* could he fly? C'mon! What I finally had to accept was that there was knowledge, wisdom, education, that didn't reduce to causal explanation. It worked within an age-old tradition of cultural living. I found my western mind butting up against stuff it just couldn't fathom; I had to take it on faith, and in good faith, if this new world was to open up to me. I'm glad I did.

That experience, one of many which started me on the journey to question my own westernized view of reality, was reinforced many times while living in Pikogan. I remember another time when another Elder in the community was talked about as having the ability to take the shape of a bear (from which we learn of the "bear-walking" tradition). A bear can move quickly, and at night; when the community was in dire need of food, the Elder would take the shape of a bear and find out where there was a mess of moose or gaggle of geese. Then he would return to the community and the hunters would go out the next day to where the bear-walker had been and find exactly what the bear-walker said they would find. Again, a gift from the Creator for the benefit of the community. These kinds of experiences sounded strange to me at first, but now they seem normal. When I again asked Wini if that particular Elder could still take the shape of a bear, he said, "Not any more.

There's no need for it. But since the white man came, some Anishnaabe began to abuse their Creator-given powers for bad things, such as seeking revenge on people, or to puff themselves up in the eyes of the community. That's why we mostly tend to fear people who can shape-shift nowadays. The Creator gave us those gifts while they were needed, and now they are no longer needed."

From the perspective of the Elders in the communities of Pikogan and Winneway, "teachers" are those who can demonstrate the relationship between philosophy and practice. It's important to remember that one's way of life is a model of what one knows. Who do people in a community seek out for advice, prayer, guidance, showing how, and so forth? Different people in a community have different powers and different ways of accessing knowledge, and therefore, have different responsibilities to those around them. During the Oka Crisis in 1999, the Mohawks talk about how an eight-year old boy became their "teacher," their "Elder," guiding them in their actions and strategies. Alanis Obansawin documented this phenomenon of the "young" being the "Elder" in her documentary, *Kanasatahke: 240 Years of Resistance*. In my own culture you have to go through years of schooling and practice in order to become a "teacher," while in most Aboriginal traditions the Creator has designed it so that both "teaching" and "being an Elder" is not age-graded. Sometimes a very young person can be a "teacher," while an

Elder may, in fact, be merely a "student." Being regarded as an "Elder" is not so much related to age as it is to the wisdom and profundity you "teach," regardless of age. The community knows who the Elders are: the ones who community members regularly go to for prayer, guidance, and advice.

As Linda Akan (1992) writes from a cultural-member's perspective:

> An Elder is regarded as someone who knows what is important in life and applies that knowledge to his or her life. The authority of an Elder comes from the recognition of this knowledge by others, and the reliability of the Elders' discourse can be tested in the context of time, when it lasts: values and attitudes that outlast conflict and contradictions are reflective of a peace-oriented paradigm that pervades the essence of "good talks." (192)

So, being a "teacher" or a "student" may depend on one's individual knowledge or experience. I remember one day in the community of Winneway, which is a semi-isolated community with lots of water around it. A bunch of us were having a meeting in a building by the river, and all of a sudden we heard yelling and screaming outside. We rushed out of the building and made our way down to a commotion by the river. A five year old child had apparently just drowned and his father, wailing and with tears in his eyes, was carrying his son up to the riverbank, yelling, "My son is dead! My son drowned." The boy had no heartbeat, wasn't breathing, and was turning blue. I remember thinking, "Hey, I've watched lots of TV shows where people give CPR. Maybe I should give it a shot!" Sure enough, I followed what I had seen on TV as best I could and within a minute or so the small boy lying on the sandy beach began to spit up water and started breathing! Many of the onlookers broke into applause and audible prayers for the Creator saving this young boy's life (even if He had to use a white guy to do it!). For many days after that incident, practically the entire community offered me gifts and thanked me for what I did. Me, I just thanked God and the generosity of the people. The point being that I had been cast into the "teacher's" role, even though I had never performed CPR in my life! Sometimes we're "teachers" and sometimes we're "students," a very common maxim in Anishnaabe thinking. I was sure glad to be at the right place at the right time—at least for once in my life! But just in case you think I got a swelled head over my life-saving heroics, I'll tell you another episode that sort of, how shall we say, balances things out.

Shognosh Goes First...

I can't remember exactly when I started keeping a list of "things the Elders found dangerous about what the young people at Pikogan weren't learning anymore," but over the years I began to pay attention to what the Elders in the community complained about when referring to the younger generation. Apart from the multitude of jokes and stories about non-Native Canadians, the Elders' stories mostly had to do with "bush skills" and how the young people were putting themselves in dangerous situations by not knowing about what those skills were. I often heard that the "young people" no longer knew how to act appropriately in the bush and how dangerous that was. And in the eleven years that we lived in the community there were a number of accidental deaths and close calls of young people in the bush without Elders around. So it was a real concern for the Elders.

One day one of the guys from the reserve, Tchoo-Tchoo, invited me to go with him to scout out places to set beaver traps. Hmm...sounds exciting, I thought. We were about the same age, still considered to be in the category of *"gaa oshkii bimaadiziwaaj"* (young people) from the Elders' perspective, and we were. We left his cabin in the bush and walked for about a mile until we reached the river. It was early spring and the ice on the river was getting a bit treacherous. We thought it would be worth crossing the river to check out some areas on the other side. My friend walked to the edge of the river, took a few steps, then beckoned me to come with him. After a few more timid steps, he took his ever-present .22 rifle and shot a hole in the ice. He got down on one knee to examine the hole. Then, satisfied that the ice was thick enough to hold us as we crossed, he said to me in his language, "Oh, yes, the ice is strong enough. You go first." I took a few confident steps and then plunged through the ice into the frigid river. Fortunately, we were still close enough to the riverbank that I was able to gain some footing and, with my friend's help, scramble back onto the ice and then off the river completely. We had a good laugh as we hurried back to his cabin (although I think he was laughing harder than I was!). And when we got back to the reserve my friend told and retold the story and it got lots of laughs, especially the part about his good fortune in sending me onto the ice first! But I learned something else from watching the elders' shake their heads at the method he had used for testing the ice.

Now, the Elders weren't above having a chuckle at Shognosh's soaking; after all it's downright hilarious when a white guy falls through the ice, right? Interestingly, though, it was Tchoo-tchoo who received the brunt of the Elders' comments, along the lines of, "Okay, so you did have a good idea by sending Shognosh onto the ice first, but, hey, we're beginning to become quite concerned that our *own* young people are forgetting how dangerous the bush can be and how important it is *to listen to us* when we tell you how to survive properly in the bush, especially in the winter." Like, when I started talking to the Elders about this incident, this is what they told me: "We would *never* use a .22 to test the strength of the ice. That's what *white* people do! It's much too dangerous. Our parents and grandparents taught us to use a big, strong stick to pound the ice in front of you to make sure that it was strong enough to walk on. And we're pretty sure we taught Tchoo-tchoo that, too, but he seems to keep forgetting our teachings! That could have cost him—and you—your lives."

9

Oral Storytelling: Keeping the Connection

In many Aboriginal traditions, oral storytelling is the most important tool for teaching and passing on the sacred knowledge and practices of the First Nation. Seems natural when you think that "…The human memory is a great storehouse ordinarily filled to only a fraction of its capacity. The Elders knew this and tested and trained the memory along with the other senses, so that the history and traditions of *The People* could be preserved and passed on (Beck, Walters and Francisco, 57).

I thought it would be a good idea to follow the chapters on Aboriginal language and traditional education by talking a bit about the oral storytelling tradition, which binds language and education together. Storytelling continues to play an important role in the lives of virtually every First Nation person today, as it has for millenia. At least, that's what I've been told by many Elder storytellers—and they should know!

In talking with people from my own non-Native tradition, I get the sense that we underestimate the strength and power of what is commonly referred to as the "oral tradition." I mean, when you get to my age you might well wonder how reliable a knowledge that depends on our frail memories can be. What we forget (geddit, *forget*, n'yuk, n'yuk) is that our culture is full of information storage technologies that make a well-developed individual memory unnecessary. So we evaluate the "oral tradition" out of our perspective steeped in a tradition of books, libraries, radio, television, the internet, and CNN. Since we consider *our* memories to be faulty we tend to think that the memories of *all* peoples are equally weak. Well, it ain't so. And by the way, who said CNN was reliable knowledge? Hmm?

Have you ever wondered what a "myth" is? You've probably used the word in everyday conversation, along with such words as misty, romantic, supernatural, realm, and adventure. But for Anishnaabe people, "myth" is not just a word used to describe "Life in a Galaxy Far, Far Away." It's a regular and normal part of the reality of most Anishnaabe people. I remember reading *The Power of Myth* by Joseph Campbell, the late mythologist, and at one point he writes:

What human beings have in common is revealed in myths. Myths are stories of our search…for truth, for meaning, for significance. We all need to tell our story and understand our story. We all need to understand death and to cope with death, and we all need help in our passages from birth to life and then to death. We need to…understand the mysterious, to find out who we are. (5)

He then puts the question to us directly:

How do you understand myth? As an outdated and primitive way of understanding the universe or as a vibrant, living carrier of truths about the universe? What are *your* myths? What stories influence the way you view the world? Nature? God? Relationships? Family? Values? (6)

So, myths are stories we tell ourselves in order to make sense of the world we live in. You know, like the Garden of Eden, or the Big Bang. But those two are origin stories, and for most of us they don't affect our day-to-day lives all that closely. But others do. Stories are all around us; though we may not be aware of it, we tell them, and live them, daily. They shape the way we act with each other. The problem is, as Campbell points out, most 21st century people are so divorced from our indigenous roots (since all of us ultimately came from an indigenous tradition somewhere down the line), that our "stories" are now largely derived from pop culture: *Star Wars* and *Lord of the Rings*, and summer blockbusters and "reality" TV shows. So it's an interesting question to ask yourself: what are your *stories*? What "stories" motivate you to live a better life, to respect the environment and other persons, be they human persons or other-than-human persons? Or do your stories tell you to ignore the environment, look out for number one, and rake in as many resources as you can get?

It's different for most Anishnaabe people. After thousands of years they aren't divorced from their roots, though the residential school assimilation plan almost succeeded in breaking the line of continuity. But it didn't! Anishnaabe people still have their stories—ancient stories often told in contemporary settings—which tell about the right way to live and what one ought to value and how to maintain healthy relationships with the environment, the Creator, and with each other. Personally, I have a hard time thinking about what *my* stories are, except from what I've learned over the years from Anishnaabe people. I think that's what I'm really referring to when I say that living with Anishnaabe people has *transformed* my life. Now I have stories! Adopted, granted, but my stories nevertheless.

Mr. Lynx goes after some Tail, and ends up with a short one

Okay, so let's take a peek at a story I heard while living in the community of Pikogan and see what we can see. This is about how the lynx wanted get rid of his long, scraggly tail and have a nice, fluffy tail like the fox. We'll look at the English translation of the legend and try to figure out what the legend is trying to teach us. Now, we'll only be looking at one story in this chapter, but believe me, the Anishnaabe tradition has hundreds of them, if not thousands, all locked up in the heads of the Elders. So the only way one can truly gain access to them is by asking the Elders. And if they are kind enough to tell you some, you first have to learn their language so that you can understand the stories properly. Gets pretty complicated, say what? But what else are you gonna do? Well, you're going to read my translation! Remember, I'm your bridge builder. I learned the language and survived to write to you about it! Of course my version won't be the same as those told in Anishnaabemowin, but you'll get the idea. Hey, the Elders *told* me to write down stories and *share* them. Remember the importance of *sharing*? So, we're both, you and me, making a gesture to acculturate. Believe me, it's appreciated.

Me, I've chosen to use a pretty short story, because they can get extremely long and complicated and, while they're still pretty cool, sometimes it takes hours just to sit and hear them (or, in our case read them). In fact, according to 4th degree Midé healer James Dumont (from Midewiwin, Great Medicine Society; a 4th degree means he's a really cool Medicine Man), the telling of the origin myth of the Anishnaabe people can take up to seven days! (Sort of like Wagner's *The Ring of the Nibelung* that takes four days to perform.) I never had the opportunity to hear the 7-day version, but I always assumed that there must be lots of potty breaks and even time for eating and sleeping a bit, but I'll have to check that out.

So…where did that story get to? Oh, here it is. It's all about how Mr. Lynx wanted to get some nice tail. And boy, does he ever get it! I should note, too, before we get started, that the Lynx in the Anishnaabe tradition at Pikogan is kind of like the Wile E. Coyote of the Anishnaabe World, always ending up the butt of the joke or the teaching—but hey, everyone has a role to play! It kind of makes me think, who is the Wile E. Coyote in Canadian stories? I dunno. The Prime Minister, maybe?…

The Lynx and the Fox

One time the lynx met up with the fox.
At that time he asked him,
"How do you get your tail to look so nice?"
The fox says, "I break a hole in the ice.
So then I put my tail where I made the hole.

So then when it's frozen I jump up really fast."
He tries it, too, that lynx,
to break the ice to make a hole.
At last that Lynx's tail is frozen.
So then he really must have jumped up when his tail was
   frozen in the hole.
Frozen to the ice.
That Lynx broke his tail off when he jumped up!
So that's why the lynx has a short tail.

So, there you go. Nice legend, say what? Now, the first thing we wanna do is try and figure out what the heck this little legend is trying to teach. Like, most of us think that culture has certain values or important things that the older generation (grandma and grandpa) want the young people to learn so that when the young people become grandmas and grandpas they can teach their grandchildren who will eventually become grandmas and grandpas themselves someday. Follow that? Anyway, it reminds me of what one Anishnaabe Elder told me in passing one day. He said, "Life is strict, but if you follow our teachings carefully, you will have a better and longer life." Right on, that Elder. Like, we want to live long and happy lives, right? So we better pay attention to what the Elders have to say. If not, well, it isn't going to be anybody's fault but your own if you live a short, crummy life. Well, maybe sometimes you can't help the short part, but you can do something about the crummy part. So anyway, what are some of the basic cultural values for Anishnaabe people that we can glean from this story?

One of the biggies is the value of *respect*. But what is respect, anyway? Like, you know Rodney Dangerfield who's always saying, "Hey, I don't get no respect!" (Well, actually, unless you're a geezer like me you probably don't know Rodney Dangerfield. Too bad what our youth today is missing…go UTube him). So what exactly is it that Rodney's not getting? Well, here's what one Elder has to say: "Don't favor one child. Love them equally. Teach them how to love, respect and value each other as individuals" (Okinawe, personal communication, 1985). Like, the lynx there wasn't happy with the way the Creator made him. He compared his own long, scraggly tail with the nice, fluffy tail of the fox. Like, after he saw the nice tail on the fox, well, he wanted one just like it. He didn't realize that it's important to *accept yourself just the way you are*. He didn't respect himself. And we're all like that sometimes, too, don't you think? We see someone else and maybe they're really good-lookin' or smart or something like that and all of a sudden we're not happy with the way we are. "Oh, if only my nose wasn't so big!" or "I sure wish I had a way with the ladies like Shognosh does!" Hey, be happy with what you got, pal! We can't all be God's gift to women… What I mean is, you might as well like yourself whether you like it or not. 'Cause that's the way it is.

What other values can we see in the story? Well, way back in chapter five I mentioned a few basic values: maintaining harmony, sharing, non-interference. And sure enough, they're in the story! Mr. Fox maintains the harmony in his relationship with Mr. Lynx by sharing his knowledge and by not interfering, even though we can be pretty sure ol' Mr Fox knew that Lynxy shouldn't be trying to get a new tail. "But wait a minute," I hope you're about to say, "that Fox just led the Lynx on. He set him up. There's no way the Fox ever froze his tail in the ice. He lied to the Lynx. How's that non-interference?" Good points! You're catching on! Right, the story is a *funny* one, at the Lynx's expense. It always evoked lots of laughter on the rez. I mean, the Lynx is a fool, right? Yet the values the community recognizes *are there*, at least in parody. The really funny part is that the Lynx can't see the fraud. He's too caught up in wanting to be something he's not.

So, the story works in a few ways at once: its basic *teaching reinforces* fundamental cultural values like self-respect and humility; its *parody reminds* the community of other important cultural values like sharing, non-interference and maintaining harmony; and it's *satiric humour binds* the community together in laughing at the foolish lynx. And when you reflect for a moment that the story of the foolish lynx has been told and retold for hundreds if not thousands of years in communities throughout Anishnaabe World, you can get a sense of how deeply ingrained its structure and rhythms are to the values it shares. The Elders don't need to tell the group the "moral" of the story. The people enter into the morality of the community as the familiar tale draws them in.

You "Lynx Clan" are so gullible!

10

Native Humour, and why Canadians often don't seem to "Get It"

Let's start with some funny stuff, okay? At least, let's see if *you* think it's funny…

In his article, "Striking the Pole: American Indian Humor," Joseph Bruchac tells an Abenaki story he heard from a Native Elder that epitomizes the nature of American Indian humour. Many years ago, the story goes, there was a white trader who had a slippery reputation. He was known for having a bad temper and for cheating the Indians when they came to trade with him. When Indians would bring in their skins to trade, the white trader would use an old-fashioned balance scale and would pay them by the pound for their skins. Instead of using a counter-weight on his scales, however, he would just place his hand on the tray and say, "My hand weighs exactly one pound." One day the Indians who came to trade with him got tired of being cheated. They purchased a set of weights and came to the trader's store to confront him with his dishonesty. The trader, angry at being accused of cheating, pulled a rifle out from underneath the counter and began shooting at the Indians. The Indians responded by firing back and the white trader was killed in the exchange of gunfire. Then, just out of curiosity, the Indians cut off his hand and weighed it on their own scales. They felt kind of bad to discover that his hand weighed exactly one pound!

Now, here's an excerpt from Aboriginal comedian Don Burnstick's shtick about "Living on the Rez":

—When you hear someone say that they are going out for a few drinks on Friday night, it really means they are going to binge until Sunday night.

—Driving around the Rez you will notice that blankets and the Indian Flag (you know which one!), are substitutes for curtains.

—At a party, laughs are guaranteed when someone passed out on the couch gets tipped over.

—At that same party, fights will break out between family members, best friends, etc. only to be forgotten a few hours later.

—You go to the local bar and notice a few kids

scattered here and there in the lobby. (A.k.a.-Lobby Kids) And they have in their hands the chips-and-gum-and-bar-and-drinks-Special.

—When you agree to baby-sit someone else's children, you end up having to look for the parents a few days later.

I find it kind of interesting how non-Natives who have heard these particular pieces react to them. While some laugh, usually the laughter is tinged with nervousness. Others don't seem to "get" the humour in them. In fact, some are quite offended by it, either taking umbrage at its treatment of white culture, or of First Nations culture. Personally, I think reactions to these pieces, and to a culture's humour generally, allow us to gauge an important truth: if you can understand what makes a people laugh, you are closer to understanding and appreciating them. If you don't *geddit*, there's a good chance you don't understand something significant about the culture. Rather than going off half-cocked, perhaps you need to pay closer attention, or at least acknowledge that you're outside a circle. But hey, surely the moral of the first little story above is the importance of sharing, or, wait for it…"lending a hand…", ba da bing, ba da boom!

My life at Pikogan and my relationships with Anishnaabe friends have shown me many times over the years that First

Nations laughter and humour are ways of dealing with a life that can be so tragic and wonderful at the same time. Like the "lending a hand" story, a good number of humorous Aboriginal stories in Canada are clearly responses to the dark history of Native/non-Native relations and are intended for a mixed Native/non-Native audience. I mean, half the impact of the story is watching the non-Native listeners get all twitchy. Another strain of Anishnaabe humour, though, is for the home crowd, or in-group (which of course doesn't mean non-Natives can't listen in). Like, all that Don Burnstick rez humour makes non-Natives wonder how anyone can laugh at it. But that's the point:

That's odd... I plugged it in last night and it still seems sluggish this morning!

if it's just us insiders partaking, then we can have a good yuk at the all-too-familiar stereotypes of the rez. But it could be a bit risky for the non-Native to start belly-laughing about those clichés. Remember what I said at the beginning of chapter one about in-group and out-group language? Well, it's like that. You gotta *earn* the right to laugh at insider jokes. Despite this, and though it was sort of weird for me at first, I never laughed so hard and so often as I did when living in the community of Pikogan.

The writings of Drew Hayden Taylor, an Anishnaabe from Curve Lake, Ontario, capture both the complexity and dynamics of Ojibwe-specific humour. Much of that humour is grounded in the history of Native people in contact with non-Natives, and Taylor seems to have a special knack for uncovering the humorous underbelly of that relationship. As you might expect, the humour works (as *lots* of humour works, regardless of culture) by smacking two different sets of values up against each other. Here's an example from Taylor's writings, on something as innocuous as breast implants:

> On the one hand, Native people have this wonderful respect and love for the land. We believe we are part of it, a link in the cycle of existence... On the White hand, there's breast implants. Darn clever of them White people. That's something that Indians would never have invented... We just take what the Creator

decides to give us. But no, not the White man. Just imagine it, some serious looking White doctor sitting around in his laboratory muttering to himself, "Big tits. Hmm, how do I make big tits?" If it was an Indian, it would be, "White women sure got big tits," and just leave it at that. ("Pretty Like a White Boy", 1996)

I often use the writings of Drew Taylor when talking with non-Native Canadians; they're thought provoking and as you've just seen there's a biting humour to them. While he's not immune to criticism from the non-Native populace, he sees it as something to be expected given the content of his humour. And finally the White reaction is sort of beside the point because he's not primarily writing for non-Natives but as part of his culture, one that has taken a certain form and has a certain history due to its interaction with Whites. For example, after Drew Taylor gave a talk on "Native Humour" some years ago to a group of secondary students in Ottawa, one student was brave enough to ask him, "How can you get away with writing what you do about white people?" His response was quite diplomatic and demonstrates what I believe is a recurrent theme in what is commonly called "Indian Humour." He responded: "In my writing, I often poke fun at the dominant culture in what I believe to be a kind-hearted, inoffensive way, as any satirist might." He continues,

It's my observation that Native humour often crosses the tenuous and ambiguous boundary between the politically correct and the politically incorrect. Native humour pushes the envelope. It [often] goes places polite and civil humour won't go. It reflects injustice and anger…and it's located somewhere between the heart, the belly and the crotch…Basically, Native humour comes from five hundred years of colonization, of oppression, of being kept prisoners in our own country. Humour keeps us sane. It gives us power. And it gives us privacy. Whenever two First Nations people get together, something magical is sure to happen: there will be laughter! Native humour is a little bit of home tucked away for when we need it. Sort of like spiritual pemmican. (Taylor, 2005: 68-69)

So, when I'm approached by non-Native people who tell me that they're offended by some of Drew's stories, I invite them to try and take off their own cultural glasses and, at least for a moment, put on *Anishnaabe* glasses and grasp a glimpse of the world through the Anishnaabe perspective. It really is a different world from a Native perspective, and I believe it's important to understand just how different, regardless of whether or not one "buys into" that perspective. Understanding the differences can go a long way in building bridges of mutual respect and understanding between Native people and non-Natives in Canada, and humour can help build those bridges, which brings us full circle, back to the important maxim we began this hilarious chapter with: if you can understand what makes a people laugh, you are closer to understanding and appreciating them.

One final word from Drew Taylor that may, in fact, save your life some day (or at least your face...); this book is, after all, a *survival guide*... In *Funny, You Don't Look Like One* (1996), Drew includes some philosophy for life on the rez, advice that "...you don't need a Ph.D. to understand."

—Never trap on another person's trap line.
—Enjoy the variety of life; that's why the Creator made four seasons.
—Family will be there when strangers won't.
—Beware of unusually coloured snow.
—Life is a circle, try not to get lost.
—Whenever you hunt an animal, make sure it's not hunting you.
—Be careful who you date, they could be your relation.
—Nobody can see tomorrow without first looking at yesterday.
—Check the authentic Indian totem pole for a "made in Korea" label.

By the way, this whole survival thing reminds me of this story about the Anishnaabe guy and the white guy walking in the bush together (okay, it was me and Normand). Anyway, the white guy says to the Anishnaabe guy, "I hope we don't see a bear out here. Bears can run faster than humans you know (big-shot, know-it-all white guy!), so we'll never be able to outrun a bear if he comes after us. So the Anishnaabe guy turns to the white guy and says, "Hey, bro, I'm not worried about running faster than a bear. I just need to run faster than *you*!" Smart dude, him.

11

So How Well Do We Understand
Native Spirituality?

Spirituality underlies every aspect of Native ethics and behaviour; it is essential to grapple with it if we want to build a bridge of understanding between Canada and Anishnaabe World. Prayer and the exercise of spiritual power are still very important aspects of Anishnaabe life and society. Healings, dreams and visions are seen as signs of both spiritual power and the presence of the Creator. In fact, people in the community refer to a foolish person or one who is seen as wasting his or her life as "One who doesn't pray," or "One who doesn't follow the path of the Creator."

The belief in the existence of the Creator is so pervasive among Anishnaabe people that there isn't even a word for "spirituality" in the language. My friends often told me that the closest word they could think of was "*bimaadiziwin*"—"A Good Life," or "A well-balanced, straight life in constant interaction with the Creator, *Kitchie Manido*, the Great Mystery." And in speaking with other linguists of Aboriginal languages in North America over the years, I have yet to find one who has ever heard of a word for "religion" in the language they've been studying. More importantly, the Elders with whom I was friends told me the same thing. "We have no word for 'religion' in our language." There seemed to be a sense that there was a fuzzy boundary between what I would commonly refer to as the "natural" and the "supernatural." According to the Elders at Pikogan, everything that existed and happened was all part of the "natural"—be it the gift of language, the ability to shape-shift, and so on. See? It's even difficult to talk about in English because so much gets lost in the translation.

The point is, while living in the community of Pikogan, I often wondered about the different realities I was surrounded by. My "world" seemed so different from Anishnaabe world. The whole area of dreams and visions, for example, created a stark contrast with my own thinking developed in the incubator of western rationalism. I know it may sound strange, but in the eleven years I spent living in the community of Pikogan, and in the years since, I've never met a Native person who doesn't believe in the Creator. And not just a belief in the existence of the Creator, but also a belief that the Creator interacts with people in their everyday lives through dreams and visions, spirit visitors, circumstances and the teachings of the Elders. The Creator and the spirit world are just assumed. That's not to say that there aren't Native people who don't believe in God or the spirit world—I imagine one might encounter those who do not—but I have yet to meet any of them. That's a lot different than in non-Native society, where a common question is, "Do you believe in God?"

From what I've been taught over the years, and, again, I invite you to compare these teachings with your own tradition and beliefs, Anishnaabe people see this life as a blend of spirits, nature and people, both human persons and other-than-human persons. All are seen to be connected by *Kitchie Manido*, the Great Mystery. All are seen to be one, inseparable and interdependent, which is why Native people often use the term "holistic." The Elders from the Swinomish First Nation put it this way:

Spirituality pervades every aspect of Indian life in ways difficult to grasp for most non-Indians.... Spirituality is not treated as a separate or discrete part of life.... It is understood to be a fundamental reality of all life and all people, inseparable, connected to physical reality, bodily events, interpersonal relations, individual destiny, mental processes and emotional well-being. (*A Gathering of Wisdoms*, 1991: 126-127)

A basic spiritual value taught to me by the Elders at Pikogan, and since confirmed over the years by many Elders from different communities and traditions, is a sense that spirits permeate matter (for lack of a better term), which can be seen in the Anishnaabe language itself, as we have already seen in chapter seven. Spirits are able to "animate" what people in my tradition would refer to as "matter" or "material" things, which unfortunately led to the early anthropological belief in *animism* among Native people in North America. Like, my guess is that if you're a Canadian reading this book this stuff is pretty new to you; you may even see it as "primitive" or "stupid" or whatever. And you certainly have a right to your opinion. As I tell my students in my Native Studies courses, you aren't evaluated on whether or not you "buy into" what I'm teaching, or "adopt" these teachings as your own. That's none of my business. But you *are* evaluated, I tell them, on how well you understand what you're being taught and how well you're able to articulate it. But, the cool thing is this: at least now you *know* what Anishnaabe people believe. And that's a start, wouldn't you agree?

Chapters eight and nine talked about traditional education and oral storytelling. I think you can probably see by now that both of these aspects of Anishnaabe life are manifestations of spirituality. Virtually every Aboriginal tradition in the Americas has its myths—traditional stories—about where the people came from and how they were created, and these myths of their origins, as they are passed on orally, also remind the people of their place in the universe. Heavy stuff, say what? These questions are at the core of Aboriginal identity and extremely important to keep vitally alive as they continue on this earth-walk (*there's* a good Native-inspired phrase for ya!). The neat thing, for me, is that I feel I had this wonderful privilege to start asking *myself* these questions. As I said earlier, living with Anishnaabe people had a truly transformative effect on my development as a person. It's like, I really think that myths *do* invest one's life with meaning, and bring the sacred into one's everyday life. I know they do for me, anyway. The best part, at least for me, is that learning these teachings helped me to keep in touch with myself and my place in the universe (although, to be fair, I still get confused at times!). But I've noticed that what I call my "spiritual" life has truly been revitalized since I began hanging out with Anishnaabe people, and I'll never be able to thank them enough for that.

Given the previous paragraph about origins and place, it's not too hard to understand the spiritual importance for Aboriginal people of their relationship to the land. An Elder once put the whole relationship to me very succinctly:

To us, the land is like the air. They are both a gift from the Creator meant for the enjoyment and benefit of all living creatures. So when white people start talking about "owning" the land, or putting a fence around it, or whatever, in our minds it sounds just plain silly. Can you put a fence around the air? Can you say, "This is *my* air, you can't breathe it?" Of course not! They are gifts from the Creator, meant to be shared by all.

Anishnaabe people don't see themselves as the "owners" of the land (heck, there isn't even a word for "ownership" in the language!). They see themselves as the trustees of the land, along with all other human beings. But trusteeship doesn't mean there is no sense of territory merely because they have not built a fence around their traditional lands. Every First Nation knows the extent of its traditional territories and has a pretty clear sense of how the land, water and other resources are to be used and respected to as not to infringe on the traditional territories used by others. Somehow, though, I get the sense that most European-based peoples don't quite see it that way … We'll see the implications of this more clearly in the next chapter, on treaties.

My Sweat Lodge Experience

To go into a detailed description of Native spiritual beliefs and practices is beyond the scope of this little survival guide, and beyond my qualifications anyway. There are lots of good books out there that can give you an understanding of the basics. What I can do, though, is recount one of my experiences of Anishnaabe spiritual practice that sort of epitomizes the challenge the non-Native has in entering Anishnaabe World. After my time at Pikogan, and working with my Anishnaabe colleagues at the university, I'm still learning about all this myself, but at least now I can try to help build bridges of understanding between Anishnaabe people and Canadians. So, let me tell you about my first experience in the sweat lodge.

I was first invited to attend a sweat lodge ceremony many years ago, and since that first time I've had the privilege of participating in a variety of different sweat lodges from a variety of different traditions and for a variety of different purposes. But for this chapter, I'd like to tell you about my first sweat lodge experience (with permission from the one who conducted that particular ceremony), in order for us to share in what, for me, demonstrates the real differences between Anishnaabe ways of praying and worshiping, and Christian ways. These differences caused me some vertigo, let me tell you! But I think I've found my footing, and want to encourage you to keep an open mind as you enter that hot, dark, little room with me.

I was brought up in the Christian tradition, basically, and really had no idea what to expect when I was invited to my first sweat lodge ceremony, which happened to be in the Anishnaabe Midé (medicine) tradition. It was a pretty cool experience (actually quite "hot," when I think about it!), but it sure surprised my assumptions about "going to church." Like, one thing I learned in the Catholic Church (besides running away whenever they asked for "altar boys"), was that you were expected to be quiet. Yeah, a 12-year old staying quiet for an hour… But you were also expected to dress up in clothes that you would never wear at any other time (except perhaps at a funeral), that were itchy and that basically constricted your breathing apparatus. Anyway, I'm telling you this to set up how different the Christian (at least Catholic Christian) way of worship was from the Anishnaabe way, both physically and spiritually.

The sweat lodge ceremony I was fortunate to attend didn't require me to don any "special" clothes—in fact once inside the sweat lodge it was clothing optional! (Something you were not likely to see at the Catholic Lodge…). Now, as with the mass in the Catholic Church, there was a certain decorum or solemnity expected, but boy, were they ever different in nature! The sweat lodge was a one-room, relatively small structure seating about 12 or 13 people, and made from natural elements:

spruce boughs, trees bent to form a circle, hides thrown over the top of the Lodge, and a pathway from the fire pit to the Lodge entrance. The fire pit contained what Anishnaabe people call "the Grandfathers," red-hot rocks which had been placed in the fire pit hours before the ceremony was to begin. There was always a Firekeeper who kept the fire going and who, when the ceremony started, would bring the "grandfathers" into the Sweat Lodge. But, hey, hold on a minute; I'm getting a bit ahead of myself here.

The sweat lodge was constructed out in the bush, a good half-mile or so from someone's house. So we first met in the house (about 12 of us, including the Conductor) so that we could hear the teaching of the "little boy"—the water drum who would accompany us into the lodge. Now, being a Shognosh (a non-cultural member), I'm still learning, so some of what you read here may be told differently by a Midé medicine man. Nevertheless, this is *my* story, and part of the learning about the sweat lodge is through my uninitiated observations.

I erroneously thought that the sweat lodge teaching would be as solemn as the Catholic Mass, and there *was* a certain solemnity to the teaching. On the other hand, I also sensed a great deal of humour and laughter as the story was told, such as, "Hey, you forgot the part about the…[whatever it was]", and "Don't forget to put the right amount of water into the little boy (the water drum)." Then, near the end of the teaching, the unthinkable happened (at least, *I* thought it was unthinkable). One of the members of the lodge had forgotten to put the plug in the water drum, and as the Conductor was testing the water drum to make sure that it was ready, water started to spill out the side of it! I was aghast, but almost everyone else had broken into gales of laughter, along with comments like, "Yeah, good job of making sure the little boy had his plug in!" and "Well, that's the last time you'll be asked to check the water drum!" In my mind, it was as if the wine had spilled on the floor during the saying of the Catholic Mass! But, no, the whole atmosphere was so different. The people at the sweat lodge knew that they were human and that the Creator, too, had a sense of humour! So they added a bit more water and plugged up the little boy, and, after a final prayer, off we went to the sweat lodge.

Now, as I mentioned earlier, the lodge was set up a good half-mile from the house, but did I tell you that it was in the middle of winter and it was about -30 degrees Celsius out? No? Well, imagine going out in your clothes, trekking a half-mile through the snow and cold, and then, upon arriving at the sweat lodge, taking all your clothes off in -30 weather! Then, before entering the lodge, each took a handful of tobacco and offered it to the grandfathers, all the while growing more and more numb in our extremities (at least *I* was!). By the time we were ready to enter the lodge, I couldn't feel my feet or hands— I mean, I *literally* couldn't feel them and had to crawl through the Lodge opening, announce my name, and find my spot where I was to sit for the next three hours.

Ah, but the good part is that, when the Firekeeper started bringing in the grandfathers, the Lodge started to heat up pretty fast. Then, after awhile, it was more than just warm, it was downright *hot!* I might as well tell you right now that by the end of the three-hour ceremony, in which we went around the lodge four times in song and prayer, I really thought I was going to die. I couldn't breathe, my brain felt like it was about to explode, and I began to experience things that I had never seen before, which put me into quite a dilemma.

You see, since I had grown up in the western way of life, my *mind* knew that the things I actually saw and experienced were physically impossible. Okay, so here was my dilemma. As one of the grandfathers was brought into the lodge, I began to understand why the Anishnaabe language refers to rocks as "living beings." You could actually see their veins as they throbbed while being brought into the lodge and placed in the pit. Then, I noticed that a sizeable chunk of one of the grandfathers had broken off. I watched carefully as the Conductor of the sweat reached his hand into the fire pit, extracted this red hot piece of rock, examined it for a good five seconds, and then tossed it out of the lodge.

I knew that what I had just observed was physically impossible—human flesh can't touch almost molten rock without it causing a blister or at least a cry from the person who picked it up. It's just not possible! I had to explain it to myself, at least, right? So, here were my options. Maybe the Conductor was somehow playing a trick on us; maybe he put some grease or something on his hand before he picked up the rock. But that didn't seem right. I *knew* these people. They weren't trying to deceive me. So I discounted that as a possibility. Okay, maybe I was hallucinating, and I suppose that's possible, although I spoke with virtually everyone else, and they had all observed what the Conductor had done and shrugged it off with "It happens all the time." So, I had one explanation left. There were laws, or rules, or *something* in this world that I didn't understand. And, truthfully, after thinking about it for a long time, that was the conclusion I came to. We live in a world of wonder and what we know to be true is vastly outweighed by what *we don't yet know how to explain*. After all, I had already dealt with people knowing how to fly and shape-shift, so it wasn't such a great leap to just shake my head and say, with Scully and Mulder, "The Truth Is Out There"…

Well, I could go on, but at least you have had a glimpse into why I'm still trying to figure it all out—especially the "ins" and "outs" of "Native Spirituality." My point is, I have been irrevocably transformed by living with Anishnaabe people, and just comparing the kinds of experiences I've had with your own might bring you into your *own* dilemma. "Is this guy nuts?"

"Well, he does have a Ph.D." "Yeah, but in what, Weirdology?"

All I can say is I've had to deal with my own dilemmas, and you'll have to deal with yours. Or not. You can just pooh-pooh all this stuff and say, "Ah, he must be on drugs." But I'm not. There's a world of wonder out there, and if you think you have a corner on the Truth, let me let you in on a little secret—*you don't!*

Must be a men's sweat tonight!!!

12

Everything You Always Wanted To Know About Treaties (But Were Afraid To Ask…)

Well, here we are at the treaty chapter, finally. I've mentioned in a few places already that there was clearly a big "misunderstanding" occurring at the time the treaties were signed. I hope that having read the previous chapters you'll now be fairly well primed to recognize how that "misunderstanding" took place. Yeah, I put those scare quotes around "misunderstanding" because it's not all that clear that *both* sides misunderstood what was going on. Words and phrases like deception, lying, 'pulling a fast one,' 'taking advantage,' start to worm their way into the discussion when you start to look into the documents. Why? Well, let's briefly recap the basic values of Anishnaabe World, values, remember, that are intrinsically spiritual: respect, maintaining harmony, sharing, non-interference, non-contradiction, wait-time, 'Indian time,' indirect requests, the importance of the oral tradition, the trustee relationship with the land. So, the Anishnaabe of Treaty 9 in Ontario, for example, carried these values into their discussion with the Treaty Commissioners. On the other side of the treaty table Duncan Campbell Scott and his fellow commissioners were motivated by policy, practicality, and written contract law. They needed to get a vast tract of land "ceded, released, surrendered and yielded up" to enable unencumbered development, the forward movement of civilization. They had to get the obstacle of Indian land title out of the way. And they had a very narrow window of time to 'close the deal' with all the bands. Further, while they were "empowered to offer certain conditions, [they] were not allowed to alter or add to them in the event of their not being acceptable to the Indians" (Scott, Report, Treaty 9). So, they could not negotiate. The terms put to the Anishnaabe were simple: take them or leave them, and do it quickly. And remember here—Anishnaabe people will do almost anything to avoid saying "no" or forcing someone else to say "no." Given the values mismatch, it looks like a disaster for the Anishnaabe waiting to happen. And it was. Everyone signed. With very few demurs. Why? Would these people have accepted a crappy deal just to avoid confrontation? Well, I don't think so. But they might have signed one they didn't really "get" in the spirit of hope, goodwill, keeping promises…and avoiding confrontation. In any event, I expect they'd be made mighty uncomfortable by the situation they were put in.

I'm going to go out on a bit of a limb here and see if I can come up with a scenario which all of us can get our heads around, a scenario which reflects the reality of the "treaty-making" process in Canada and how, if everyone plays by the same rules, the treaty-making process can be the first huge step in creating a level playing field for both Canadians and First Nations. (A "treaty" is defined by the United Nations as a promise between two nations in which each party is required to keep their part of the bargain. *Quel surprise!*)

Imagine this:

Treaty Commissioners talking to First Nations representatives:

Hey, you guys have all this cool land that, really, you don't do all that much with as far as we can tell [meaning: you certainly aren't using it the way *we* would]. So, how about this? If you promise to extinguish all rights to your land, then *we* promise you that we will take care of all your basic needs for as long as the grass grows and the rivers run. Yep, we'll provide you with all the educational opportunities you need, all your housing needs, food (you'll get to hunt and fish exactly like you do now), money ($8.00 each on signing and $4.00 per year forever afterwards. Generous, say what?)—you name it, you got it. And the deal is that all you have to do is *extinguish your land rights*! How's that for a deal? It's like we're giving you the deal of a lifetime! Now let's shake hands and we'll call it a "treaty." So, whaddya say?

The First Nations representatives scratch their heads, huddle for awhile, then respond:

Whadda we say? We say, "Screw You!" You'll never get any respectable First Nation to sign a document that calls for the *extinguishment* of our land rights! Are you nuttier than a fruitcake? How can we extinguish what we don't own? Sheesh, we don't even know what owner-ship means! But we do know we belong here. We do know the Creator wants us to look after the land— respect it, ya know? Like, that's why the Creator put us here. But hey, we know about *sharing*. Tell you what, let's agree that the treaties we make will be "land-sharing" agreements between Canada and us First Nations. Are you hip to that? But when you start talking about *extinguishing our rights to the land*, well, our white brothers, *forget it*! How about this: let *us* write the treaties

in *our* languages, and then *we'll* tell *you* what they mean.
Sounds fair enough, right? I mean, that's what *you're*
already doing with us. So, do we have a deal?

Okay, so I'm trying to put a highly complex historical
situation into ultra-simple terms. But, hey, we're just trying to
figure out what went wrong, right? So let's stay with it and see
where it goes.

Treaty Commissioners huddle and talk among themselves:
"Okay, we'll tell them the treaties use the phrase *land-sharing*,
but the treaty articles, which they can't read, will say *extinguishment
of all land rights*. Like, they won't even know until it's too late
that we bamboozled them! They're dying off anyway, so soon
there won't be any 'Indian Problem.'" So that's what they do.
After a few decades go by, the Canadian government starts
making lots of money off the land—cutting down trees and
selling the wood while they build stuff with the rest of it, killing
off tons of animals so they can make these nice fur hats from
beavers and other vicious critters to sell back in Europe, and
even finding precious minerals by doing a little digging into the
land: gold, nickel, even diamonds. So everyone benefits, right?
Wrong! Like, since the "treaties" were considered to be *land-
sharing agreements* from a First Nation perspective, then it makes
sense that the First Nations would also benefit from all the
goodies that are being found on and under the land, right? After

all, it was promised in the treaties, so...hey, wait a minute! That's not what happened! What the hell's going on here? Well, we already know. The treaty language, written in English and interpreted by Canadian politicians, deceived the First Nations Chiefs into thinking that they *were*, in fact, "land-sharing" agreements, when in fact the treaty language called for the *extinguishment* of all Aboriginal rights to the lands and the money made off those lands. Good deal for Canada—not so good for the First Nations.

What's that? You think I'm making this up? You don't think my scenario reflects what went on? Okay, there may be a *bit* of poetic license in there, and I know I'm no Shakespeare, but there really were some shenanigans, with devastating long term consequences. Okay, okay, read for yourself:

Exhibit A: a few excerpts from Duncan Campbell Scott's report to the Superintendent of Indian Affairs in 1905, summarizing the Treaty 9 process;

Exhibit B: a few excerpts from the actual Treaty 9 Articles.

A. From the Report:

> [The Indians at Osnaburg] were then told that it was the desire of the commissioners that any point on which they required further explanations should be

freely discussed, and any questions asked which they desired to have answered.

Missabay, the recognized chief of the band, then spoke, expressing the fears of the Indians that, if they signed the treaty, they would be compelled to reside upon the reserve to be set apart for them, and would be deprived of the fishing and hunting privileges which they now enjoy.

On being informed that their fears in regard to both these matters were groundless, as their present manner of making their livelihood would in no way be interfered with, the Indians talked the matter over among themselves [and went on to sign the next day.]...

...Moonias [from Fort Hope], one of the most influential chiefs, asked a number of questions. He said that ever since he was able to earn anything, and that was from the time he was very young, he had never been given something for nothing; that he always had to pay for everything that he got, even if it was only a paper of pins. "Now," he said "you gentlemen come to us from the King offering to give us benefits for which we can make no return. How is this?" Father Fafard thereupon explained to him the nature of the treaty, and that by it the Indians were giving their faith and allegiance to the King, and for giving up their title to a large area of land of which they could make no use, they received benefits that served to balance anything that they were giving.

B. From the Treaty 9 Articles:

His Majesty the King hereby agrees with the said Indians that they shall have the right to pursue their usual vocations of hunting, trapping and fishing throughout the tract surrendered as heretofore described, subject to such regulations as may from time to time be made by the government of the country, acting under the authority of His Majesty, and saving and excepting such tracts as may be required or taken up from time to time for settlement, mining, lumbering, trading or other purposes.

It is further agreed between His said Majesty and His Indian subjects that such portions of the reserves and lands above indicated as may at any time be required for public works, buildings, railways, or roads of whatsoever nature may be appropriated for that purpose by His Majesty's government of the Dominion of Canada, due compensation being made to the Indians for the value of improvements thereon, and an equivalent in land, money or other consideration for the area of the reserve so appropriated.

So, I wasn't too far off, was I? What's that great French word? *Legerdemain!* Sleight of hand. No wonder we need lawyers to help us read the fine print. But imagine if that fine print was in another language, one embodying values foreign to you. Whew! What's the saying? "Like taking candy from a baby...." As Scott says to his government handlers at the end of his Report, "When the vast quantity of waste and, at present, unproductive land, surrendered is considered, these allotments [for reserves] must, we think, be pronounced most reasonable." Ba da bing ba da boom.

People from any culture can quickly turn into greedy sons-of-bitches whenever money comes into play, and that, basically, is what happened on one side of the agreement—the side representing the Canadian government. Now, I could go on and on with more dates and quotations from documents and all that academic stuff, but I'm gonna leave that up to those of you who still don't believe my characterization of what *really* happened and why.... No, wait, hold on; I can't help it. I've gotta give you just two more quotations to whet your appetite for what you'll find in the full documents if you want to look further. First, here's our friend Duncan Campbell Scott the Treaty 9 Commissioner, from his essay "The Last of the Indian Treaties," written when he'd risen to be Deputy Superintendent of Indian Affairs:

To individuals whose transactions had been heretofore limited to computation with sticks and skins our errand must indeed have been dark.

They were to make certain promises and we were to make certain promises, but our purpose and our reasons were alike unknowable. What could they grasp of the pronouncement on the Indian tenure which had been delivered by the law lords of the Crown, what of the elaborate negotiations between a dominion and a province which had made the treaty possible, what of the sense of traditional policy which brooded over the whole? Nothing. So there was no basis for argument. The simpler facts had to be stated, and the parental idea developed that the King is the great father of the Indians, watchful over their interests, and ever compassionate. (*The Circle of Affection* 115)

Secondly, here's Chief Munroe Linklater of the Moose Factory Band, addressing the Royal Commission on the Northern Environment in 1978. "It is apparent," he says,

That forever and a day for all intents and purposes it is obvious to whoever reads these journals of the treaty party and history in the making, that His Majesty's treaty party commissioners perpetrated legal fraud in a very sophisticated manner, upon unsophisticated, unsuspecting natives. We have well recognized and undisputed rights to these aboriginal lands. (12)

Believe me, after you do your own research you'll wonder how Canada got away with it and keeps getting away with it.

A few years back I happened to run into Ovide Mercredi at a conference and I had the opportunity to ask him a question: "When you were National Chief of the Assembly of First Nations, how did you respond when people asked 'What do you Indians want us to *give* you so that you'll stop all your ranting and raving?'" Typical Canadian question, I thought, and one that I myself had heard many, many times over the years. But Ovide is a smart dude, and his response to me was, well, I thought it was profound. He said (and I paraphrase here),

I usually tell the person who asks me that question something like this. We don't want Canada to *give* us *anything*. What we would like Canada to do is *recognize* what currently exists and what has never been taken away from us: the God-given right to self-government (that is, to manage our own affairs in our own territories). It all goes back to the treaty-making process. And the way to rectify the situation is actually quite simple. *Canada, first keep your part of the bargain in the treaties that you have made with First Nations (which your own Human Rights Commission chastises you for not doing year after year), and second, where treaties do not yet exist, make them!*

What he was saying was, indeed, quite simple. Anishnaabe people do not look to the *Constitution Act* or acts of charity as the sources for recognizing their right to self-determination and self-government. Their sovereignty as the First Nations in Canada is an inherent gift from the Creator, and their occupancy of this land since time immemorial attests to this right. As I pointed out in the spirituality chapter, the land itself cannot be "owned." Like the air, it is a gift from the Creator for the use of every human being; an inalienable right:

When we signed treaties, the government held back or "reserved" certain lands for our own people… Also, at the time of treaty-making, our ancestors held back or "reserved" certain rights and powers of Indian Governments. These are not mentioned in the Treaty Articles, because they were not subject to negotiation. They were, and they remain, our inalienable rights. Among these are the inherent sovereignty of Indian nations, the right to self-determination, jurisdiction over our lands and citizens and power to enforce the terms of the Treaties. (*First Nations Family Justice, Awasis Agency of Northern Manitoba*. 1997:168)

In "Solutions We Favour For Change" (*Drumbeat*, 1989), former National Chief of the AFN George Erasmus sums up a common vision of First Nations people:

> We cannot afford to be pessimistic. Our people have retained, with what many observers have described as extraordinary tenacity, the central core of our beliefs, values, and cultures. We have no doubt about our continued survival, far into the future. We have always been here and we are not going anywhere. The Canadian political system will eventually have to treat us as a permanent, and important, part of this country. (295)

Despite the strategy of assimilation, despite the residential schools, despite the Apartheid system, First Nations people have never given up. And you know? An oddly funny thing has been happening over the past 30 years or so. First Nations people have become the fastest-growing population in Canada, and as they were growing they weren't very happy about the Canadian government's position of not keeping their part of their treaty obligations. In fact, they were downright pissed off, and since more and more Anishnaabe people had been educating themselves about the white man's laws and ways of doing things, even becoming lawyers and doctors and all sorts of neat things, they decided to put their foot down and demand, with support from the international community, that Canada suck it up and start keeping their parts of the bargains where treaties had already been made and make treaties where none yet existed. You see, the fatal miscalculation by the Canadian government was this: *these people didn't die off!* And now they're expanding at alarming rates! At least, alarming from a Canadian perspective. Won't that be great in fifty years or so? Canada will be a different country. Just watch! There's lot of work to be done, of course, and First Nations people welcome all allies, regardless of colour or stature or sexual orientation, in their ongoing quest for— remember?—yes, recognition of what already exists and what has existed for thousand of years.

APTN has a new Indian survival show... They take all the politicians in Ottawa and one by one vote them off an island... Turtle Island!

13

Shognosh Stories

That last chapter was heavy. Sorry. I won't say *too* heavy, because the weight of the unfulfilled treaties on the necks of the First Nations can't be overstated. Still, my sprightly step and teasy/pleasy tone in the rest of the book (okay, in *most* of the rest of the book), sorta got sidelined in chapter 12. Well...I'm back! Since I've talked a lot about the importance of story telling and traditional education and spirituality and politeness and different cultural values in this wee tome, I thought as we approach the end that I'd walk the walk a bit. So, here are two stories that recount experiences I had on the rez at Pikogan. You can look at them in two ways: as a relaxing reward for you for putting up with all the 'splainin' I've been doing thus far; or, as a test—to see if you can identify all the Anishnaabe values embedded in them. So whether you're a type A or B personality, I've got you covered.

Getting Lost? Or Finding Myself?

Once upon a time (but believe me, this ain't no fairy tale) three of us went out moose hunting by canoe for a few days. Well, after three days waaay out in the bush (or so I thought, anyway), we had never even heard a moose, had never got a shot off, but on our way canoeing back up the river, my buddy leans over and says, "Well, we really had a great time, anyway!" A great time? *I* didn't have a great time! I was tired and hungry and *we didn't kill a moose!* But when I really started thinking about it, I thought, "Y'know, we really *did* have a great time. We had lots of good conversations, I learned a lot more of their language, and they taught me stuff I thought I'd never learn about, never even *think* about, like cooking moose liver over an open fire in the bush (we had brought the liver with us, just in case!), and how to paddle a canoe and keep it going in the direction you wanted it to go (no mean feat, believe me!). But the funniest part of the trip, and most culturally disorienting, was what happened *next*.

As we were paddling back up the river, I started thinking that I hadn't heard anyone making plans about how we were to get back to the community once we made it back to the bush road. I didn't recall anyone asking someone to pick us up or saying when we might be back or...*because no one had!* Ah, but that didn't mean that they didn't have a plan. A plan involving Shognosh (me). A plan that didn't seem too well thought out (well, at least not in *my* mind). Anyway, here's what happened. Evidently they knew where they were, having travelled this river and trekked in this part of the bush for many years. So Sandy (one of the Anishnaabe guys who had "arranged" the trip), paddled the canoe over to the side of the riverbank, turned to me and said, "Shognosh, jump out and follow the path and it will take you to the highway. It's only about four miles away. Then hitchhike down to the nearest gas station and when you get there, call my brother and tell him to come pick us up at the bridge at the end of the bush road." Hmm...this was starting to get a bit complicated, I thought. And, of course, the first thing I did after Sandy told me that was to say, "*What* path? I don't *see* any path!" My Anishnaabe buddies in the boat looked at each other in amazement and said, "You don't see that path? A *baby* could follow that path!" Not to be outdone (I mean, I still had *some* pride left), I said, "Okay, hope this works!"

Within half an hour the scenario went something like this: some half-crazed, sweaty, scared, white madman was thrashing his way through the bush, all the while whimpering, "I don't see a path..." in a tone that would bring tears to your eyes (and had already brought them to mine). But, suddenly, off in the distance, I heard what I thought was the faint sound of a logging truck. Could I possibly be getting close to the highway? Yes! They were right! Even a *baby* could follow this path. Long (long) story short, I made it to the highway, hailed down a passing logging truck (or did I actually throw my body in front of it?), and hitchhiked down to the nearest gas station where I got out, thanked the truck driver, and proceeded to call back to the community and get hold of Sandy's brother. I asked him if he could pick us up and he said, "Sure," and hung up. Wait, don't hang up! I didn't tell you where we…oh, forget it. And, you know, it all worked out exactly as Sandy had planned it. The only thing he *didn't* know was how close he had come to having a dead white man on his hands, lying on the ground with a death-smile frozen on his curled-up lips…

Go Team?

After about two years living in Pikogan I was getting pretty good at speaking the language (if I do say so myself). Given my facility (nice word, eh?), the Elders figured that I must also know how to *use* the language appropriately. Well, sometimes I did…but sometimes I didn't. An interesting thing happened that clued me into something I had never realized about the Anishnaabe sense of the *power* of language. I used to be a pretty athletic guy (now I mostly play Wii golf…), and when I lived at Pikogan I was in pretty good shape, could run faster than a rabbit, and was a helluva good softball and soccer player. Since most of the guys my age and younger were always keen on "playing" most sports, and since the community of Pikogan is only ten minutes away from a fairly large French town called Amos, we would usually get teams together to play in the various town leagues. Let's see, we played hockey, soccer, softball, volleyball—and some other sports, too, which I tend to forget in my old age. Anyway, since I was so fast, they would have me play center on the soccer team, but since I didn't skate very well, I usually rode the bench on the hockey team. No biggie. It was just nice being part of the "gang" and listening to and learning the language, and solidifying my friendships. Anyway, the first year we played in the town hockey league there were about eight teams, with us, of course, being the only Anishnaabe team. So, not to give the story away too quickly (and the value that we can learn from it!), we weren't very good. Our record for the first season was 1 and 27—that's right, we won one game and lost 27—and the only reason we won that one game is because the other team failed to show up for it, so we won by default. But, hey, a win is a win, right?

Anyway, we almost won a game legitimately—until Shognosh (that would be me) opened his big mouth and, believe it or not, *caused* us to lose a game in the last minute. For some reason we were leading 3-2 in the third period. Now me, I'm all excited and rooting my buddies on, but everyone else was real quiet. Hmm…I wondered about that. And most of the guys on the bench had their heads down, staring at the ground. I thought (in my best Shognosh way), "Hey, we should all be cheering our teammates on—we could actually *win* this game!" I mean, we were leading by one goal with about 90 seconds to go! So in my own inimitable Shognosh way, I jumped up, looked down the row at my teammates on the bench and loudly yelled (in Anishnaabemowin, of course), "*Kii-gii-baakinagemin!*" (which means, "We Won!"). Now, I know the game wasn't over yet, and I do tend to be an excitable boy, but I think pretty much everyone on the bench looked over at me and at least one person said, "*Kibaan kidoon!*" (loosely translated as "Shut the fuck up!"). I was a bit taken aback, since I thought I was trying to spur my buds on to victory… Well, you know what's comin' I bet.

Riiiiight. It's almost unbelievable to think about now, but within 30 seconds the opposing team tied the score and twenty seconds later scored again to take the lead, 4-3. Then the buzzer sounded and the game was over.

Well, we shuffled into the locker room, no one saying anything. But when we were all in there, someone said in a very loud stage whisper, "Shognosh lost the game for us." What!? I wasn't even on the ice and I was cheering like a maniac and *I* lost the game? Well, again, thank God for cultural friends, because no one was talking to me as we showered and drove back to the rez. But the next day I was still feeling pretty uncomfortable with that "Shognosh lost the game for us" line, so I just had to go see my friend Alfred and ask him what the hell was gong on. Now, Alfred didn't put it in academic or cultural value terms, he just said, "You really did lose the game for us because when you said 'We won!' you were very *rude* to the grandfathers and other spirits who may have been there, too." In other words, there's a very strong sense that words have power, or magic, or *something*. Words aren't just words and they must be used carefully and with respect. So my using the future tense as I did by saying, "We won!", somehow jeopardized some ongoing process in the world of power. I don't know how else to put it, but I asked a lot of people about the power of words and language after that experience, and I always got pretty much the same answer as what Alfred told me that day—

"What you say can change things. You should really learn to be respectful of words and language if you want to learn how to think like an Anishnaabe." Man, that really hurt, but I took his teaching to heart; I believe he was giving me a glimpse of something very powerful and very, I guess you could say *secretive*, about his culture. I still screw up every now and then.

If this is the "Road to the Stanley Cup"...
I think our teams desperately need a map!!!

14

Ovide Speaks, We Listen

I hope you've enjoyed the ride, dear reader (dear reader? Where the hell did *that* come from?). Yeah, we've shared some laughs, maybe even some tears (yeah, right…). Most of all, I hope we've become more informed, more educated, about First Nations people. Heck, they ain't going anywhere, so you might as well make the best of it. And I promise you, if you're a Canadian and you take one small step towards understanding Native people, you will be welcomed with open arms and big smiles. I mean, *Anishnaabe World* is my attempt, in a very respectful way, to accomplish what the Elders at Pikogan always hoped I would accomplish. It was usually said like this: "Shognosh, the Creator sent you to live with us for a purpose—

to learn not only our language but our ways of thinking and doing things. Always treat those ways with respect, as gifts from us and the Creator, and share them with your own people, when you believe it's appropriate, so that they, too, can come to understand our ways of thinking." Well, it was always said in Anishnaabemowin, so I'm not sure I'm doing it justice, but I've shared these things with you in this book out of respect for the Elders, the Creator, and all Anishnaabe people I've come to know and love over the years.

You know, it's been a lot of fun writing *Anishnaabe World*, and watching the distinctive humour of the two cultures getting to know each other emerge from the hands of Perry McLeod-Shabogesic and Tim Steven. But doing this book has also produced a lot of blood, sweat and tears. First Nations people have literally changed my life—for the better and I hope to God that this book will have a similar effect on you, *dear* reader. There is so much we can learn from Anishnaabe people in this country of Canada if we would just take the time to listen.

The Last Word, Really...

It's appropriate that I leave the final words to an Elder. And who better than my close friend Ovide Mercredi, former National Chief of the Assembly of First Nations, Chief of his reserve in Manitoba, one of the Fathers of Confederation, *really*, and, of course, a wonderful man with the best smile you're likely to see from someone who has been so misunderstood and mistrusted by Canadians over the years. Sure, he still has a wicked slice when he plays golf. Yet he smiles. From ear to ear. I love the guy, and I think you will too if you ever get the chance to meet him. But next best to meeting him is hearing him, and this last chapter is meant to provide him with a forum to be heard and you with an opportunity to hear him. I hope you really listen to what he is saying. Now *is* the right time. Our very survival as a country may depend on it.

The words you are about to read were spoken a few years ago as a convocation address Chief Mercredi gave at Carleton University in Ottawa, Ontario, and are reproduced here with his permission. You won't hear from me again, other than to say—hey, thanks for buying the book! *Gichii-miigwetch* (Thanks, brothers and sisters).

We Now Present To You, Chief Ovide Mercredi

When I was first asked to address this august body, the title that the Creator kept putting in my head was: "Indian Self-Government and Indian Sovereignty." And who wants to go two out of three with the Creator? So here it is.

The issue of sovereignty in terms of self-rule for a people is not so much a legal or constitutional issue, but a moral and political problem for all Canadians. I say this not to be disrespectful to you, but to give you a perspective which you may not have heard before.

The structure of the constitutional talks over the years has been grounded in legal and constitutional debate, and did not address the primary issue, which in my view is moral and political.

Let me explain it this way. You have a right to freedom which you cherish. You understand it thoroughly in the context of individual freedom, and you will do anything to defend it. But the individual right to freedom does not stand by itself. It derives from a collective right of freedom that we have as equals, and when you look within your own history in this country since Confederation, you have fought for and defended your freedom in two World Wars. But it wasn't the individual right that you were defending, but the collective right of freedom to your institutions of government, to your democracy.

What I fail to understand, as an Aboriginal person, is how you cannot somehow translate that passion which you have for freedom into our context as Aboriginal people.

All that we are looking for is what you already have.

All that we are looking for is what you enjoy as a people, which are your institutions that you collectively agree to, such as parliament, such as provincial legislatures, such as your judicial system. You take these institutions, not for granted, but you accept them as the collective expression of your freedom as a people. So when we, as Aboriginal people, talk about the right of self-government, we are not talking about the right that you have to tell me, and my people, how we are to conduct our affairs or how we are to live our lives. I don't agree that you have the right to tell me, as an Aboriginal person, how I have to live my life. There lies the moral issue. When we try to enter into dialogue with your government, your government continually puts obstructions in front of us about how we must rely on the rule of law. But as the Original People in this country, we ask, "Who made those rules? We didn't. We've had our own rules for thousands of years." So when your government refuses to talk to us about the "rule of law," then it becomes a political issue.

Where we are heading right now in this country is a collision course where you and I would both lose, where there will be no winners. What we have to do is to take lessons from our ancestors, both yours and mine. Those who had at least a vision that the proper way to deal with the First Nations is through discussion, negotiations, and the making of treaties. In this country there was no Indian war between us and the government of Canada (other than the resistance of the Métis people in Saskatchewan). There has never been a deployment of the army in this country against Aboriginal people until Oka. That happened, in my view, because people are losing the vision that both your ancestors and my ancestors had—that we should resolve our differences through political discussion, and that we should come to some consensus on the issues that we face together.

We have a rich heritage in this country, a very rich heritage—the treaty-making process. Why is it that contemporary Canadians and their governments have forgotten about this? Is it because you are so ethnocentric in your views that you fail to see that the actions of your government amount to white supremacy? That is a strong suggestion. But think about it. From my perspective as an Aboriginal person, when I am told, as I have been told by officials in your government, that they will not engage in discussions on the right to self-government until there is a Constitutional Amendment that recognizes explicitly our right to govern ourselves, then I know there is a great obstacle that I cannot do anything about. When we engage in discussions with your government and we try to move issues forward, they place before us the suggestion that there are only two jurisdictions in this country; the provincial government and the federal government, and you wonder to yourself: at what point in our history as Aboriginal people, as the Original People of this land, did we surrender the right to govern ourselves? Where in our history is there a document that tells you that we, as First Nations, gave you the right to tell us how we are to live? Where in our entire history is there a scrap of paper that suggests that our people have abandoned our right to exist as distinct and sovereign people?

I will tell you what sovereignty is not, so that you will at least have some understanding of why we, also, like you, cherish our freedoms. First of all, it is not The Indian Act. It is not parliament sitting down and deciding to pass a law that tells me that I can do this, but that I cannot do that. That is not sovereignty, that is not self-government, and that is not self-rule. That is someone telling you what you can or cannot do. Our people are operating under a system of government that is not traditional. The reason for that is that somewhere after Confederation, some of your people decided in Parliament that they would impose a system of government on Aboriginal people—the Chief and Council System—where they delegate powers to the Indian people, but they would not recognize the law-making ability of the First Nations. That is not sovereignty. That is delegated authority, and our people have rejected it.

When we had discussions during the Constitutional process, many of the premiers, including the Prime Minister, were totally amazed at our assertion that we have a continuing right, a pre-existing right, to govern ourselves. The source of our authority comes from the people, our own history, our own nations, and, ultimately, the Creator. Do you understand this simple truth? All we want is to express ourselves in the same way that you are able to do.

When we speak about self-government, our biggest problem in dealing with politicians, the premiers, and the Prime Minister, is that somehow it is absurd for us to think that we can govern ourselves, that it is absurd for us to imagine or even dream about government powers equivalent to provincial or federal powers. The main reason why people feel, in my view, that it is not permissible for us to express ourselves through our own institutions is the conclusion that we are not ready to govern ourselves. This is a moral issue and has nothing to do with law or constitutional change. When you form opinions about us that we are still not ready to govern ourselves, as your government has done, but that we still need a department of Indian Affairs to nudge us along, then you can appreciate what I am trying to say to you—that is not a constitutional problem, it is not a legal problem, it is a moral problem.

What do we need to do? First, we need to come to some common understanding on how we are going to co-exist in this country. We need to talk about how we are going to share the resources of this country. We need to get away from the paternalistic notion that you can have your systems of government but that we cannot. We need to talk about how we are going to share power.

Second, you have a very rich heritage as a democracy. Many of us have studied your government. We know you much more than you know us, because we are, like you, a product of your educational system. We have studied Western civilization; we have memorized in your schools the historical events of your people. We know you exceedingly well, and we know that you cherish law and order, that you cherish your freedoms.

Yet we are offended when the Attorney-General of Ontario tells the Indian lawyers that it is not possible to have Indian Tribal Courts. I say to you: When did you become the standard for human rights? Perhaps we can do better if we create our own courts. Perhaps we will interpret individual rights in a social context so that it is not possible for a person who is found guilty not to be accountable for the harm committed. Give us a chance to deal with issues such as social problems in the courts. Your courts refuse to take on that added responsibility because your lawyers and judges are on a pedestal in your society, and they cannot condescend to deal with the social problems they find in court; they leave that to social workers and psychologists.

There is something to be said for you to abandon your tendency to put obstacles in our path to self-government, because what might happen, very possibly, is that we might create laws, we might create courts, that would become models, and new standards where human rights might have different expressions and meanings. So don't throw your Charter of Rights and Freedoms at us as an obstacle. To think there is only one way of looking at human rights is very ethnocentric.

Ovide Speaks, We Listen

When I went to Geneva on the rights of the Child, when the convention was being drafted in its final stages, I was very surprised that the Western civilizations are still bullying totally everybody in the world and imposing their concepts of the "rights of the child" without taking into account the different cultures that exist. What I saw was not an exchange as I expected. My question is how a dominant society can possibly justify continuing to bully the Aboriginal people to toe the line and to be like everybody else, because it is in their best interest.

So what is it, exactly, that we want? We are looking for a way of arriving at consensual arrangements so that we can peacefully co-exist, where you can respect my collective rights as we respect yours, so that individual rights can be enjoyed by me in your society as you ought to be able to enjoy them within the context of my society as well. That is what we have to work for. That is where we have to go in the next few decades.

I may have sounded preachy at times. Sometimes I get that way. But let me tell you a story that really struck me the other day. Like you, I have to get ready for winter and I was working outside. My daughter, who looks very much Indian, was playing with some of the kids from the neighborhood—two white boys and a young girl, named Jill, who is very impressed with me! Every opportunity she gets she introduces me to her friends as one of the Indian leaders in Canada. On this occasion, she said to the boys, "He is one of the top Indian leaders in the world!"

Then, one of the white boys asked, "Then why isn't he in jail?" I didn't interfere with them, but I heard the little girl, Jill, say, "You just don't understand."

What we have to do is to make sure that we understand each other. I know you because I have studied you and studied with you. It would be nice if somehow you would force yourselves to explore us, to understand us, and maybe there's hope for this country so that, a hundred years from now, there will be another Indian leader standing here, proclaiming, not denouncing, the greatness of this country.

References

Akan, Linda. (1992). "Pimosatamowin sikaw kakeequaywin: Walking and Talking—a Saulteaux Elder's View of Native Education." *Canadian Journal of Native Education*, Vol. 19, No. 2, pp. 191-214.

Awasis Agency of Northern Manitoba. (1997). *First Nations Family Justice.* Thompson, Manitoba: Awasis Agency of Northern Manitoba.

Beck, Peggy, Anna Walters, and Nia Francisco. (1993). *The Scared: Ways of Knowledge, Sources of Life.* Tsaile, Arizona: Navajo Community College Press.

Burnstick, Don. (2008). *Ever Sick.* http://www.donburnstick.com

Campbell, Joseph. (1988). *The Power of Myth.* New York: Doubleday.

Canada, Royal Commission on Aboriginal Peoples. (1996). *Report of the Royal Commission on Aboriginal Peoples.* 5 vols. Ottawa: Canada Communications Group.

Churchill, Ward. (2001). *A Little Matter of Genocide: Holocaust and Denial in the Americas 1492 to the Present.* Boulder: City Lights Publishers.

Dobyns, Henry. (1966). "Estimating Aborignal American Populations." *Current Anthropology*, No. 7.

Dumont, James. (1992). "Journey to daylight land: through

Ojibway eyes." In David R. Miller, et. al. (eds.), *The First Ones: Readings in Indian/Native Studies.* Saskatchewan Indian Federated College Press, pp. 75-80.

Erasmus, George. (1989). "Solutions We Favour for Change." In *Drumbeat: Anger and Renewal in Indian Country.* Toronto: Summerhill Press and the Assembly of First Nations.

Hobsbawm, Eric. (1983). *The Invention of Tradition.* Cambridge: Cambridge University Press.

Lipstadt, Deborah. (1993). *History on Trial.* Cambridge: Harper Perennial.

Matthew, Marie. (2000). *The Cost of Quality First Nations Education* Vancouver: First Nations Education Steering Committee (FNESC). www.fnesc.ca

Mercredi, Ovide and Mary Ellen Turpel. (1996). *Into the Rapids.* Montreal: McGill-Queen's University Press.

Milloy, John. (1999). *A National Crime: The Canadian Government and the Residential School System, 1879-1986.* Winnipeg: University of Manitoba Press.

Paris, Erna. (2000). *Long Shadows: Truth, Lies and History.* Toronto: Alfred A Knopf.

Postl, Bill. (2004). *British Columbia First Nations Schools Funding Analysis: 2003/04 School Year.* Vancouver: First Nations Education Steering Committee. www.fnesc.ca

Ross, Rupert. (1992). *Dancing With A Ghost: Exploring Indian Reality.* Ottawa: Octopus.

References

Scott, Duncan Campell. (1905). "Report on *Treaty 9* to the Honourable Superintendent General of Indian Affairs." *Treaty 9*. Indian and Northern Affairs Canada. http://www.ainc-inac.gc.ca/al/hts/tgu/tr9-eng.asp

Scott, Duncan Campell. (1947). *The Circle of Affection and Other Pieces in Prose and Verse*. Drawings by Thoreau MacDonald. Toronto: McClelland and Stewart.

Steckley, John and Bryan Cummins. (2001). *Full Circle: Canada's First Nations*. Toronto: Prentice-Hall.

Swinomish Tribal Mental Health Project. (1991). *A Gathering of Wisdoms*. Tacoma, Washington: Swinomish Tribal Community.

Taylor, Drew Hayden. (1996). *Funny, You Don't Look Like One: Observations From a Blue-Eyed Ojibway*. Penticton, B.C.: Theytus Books.

Taylor, Drew Hayden. (2004). *Funny, You Don't Look Like One (Two)*. Vancouver: Theytus Books.

Taylor, Drew Hayden. (2005). *Me Funny*. Toronto: Douglas and McIntyre.

Treaty 9. (1905-1906). "Articles." Indian and Northern Affairs Canada. http://www.ainc-inac.gc.ca/al/hts/tgu/tr9-eng.asp

Annotated Suggested Readings

Brizinski, Peggy. (1989). *Knots In A String*. Saskatoon:
University of Saskatchewan.

    Peggy Brizinski's book takes us on an odyssey of discovery into Aboriginal views of creation, origins and mythology. Exploring a number of Aboriginal traditions, she identifies three common features of Aboriginal myths: (1) Mythic Time, (2) Mythic Characters, and (3) Mythic Structure, and helps us to grasp the meaning of Aboriginal myth, how myths fuel a people's behaviour and view of the world, and what scientists from the western tradition can learn from Aboriginal myths.

Burger, Julian. (1990). *Gaia Atlas of First Peoples; A Future for the Indigenous World*. Toronto: Anchor Books.

    Burger helps us to understand the indigenous perspectives on first contact leading up to modern colonialism, how this first contact is seen as "invasion" by indigenous peoples, and how this contact has led to the cultural and physical genocide of aboriginal peoples around the world—a phenomenon still taking place in the 21st century.

Chamberlin, J. Edward. (2004). *If This Is Your Land, Where Are Your Stories?* Toronto: Vintage Canada.

Chamberlin argues that throughout the ages First Nations stories, legends and myths have given shape and meaning to their sense of "who they are," both as cultures and nations. Not until we have thought through the meaning of "them" and "us," he argues, can we truly begin to understand each other.

Dickason, Olive. (2006). *A Concise History of Canada's First Nations*. Toronto: Oxford University Press.

Dickason, a Métis scholar, reminds us that "history" for First Nations did not begin at contact with European-based peoples. Hers is one of the first books to trace the stories of the First Nations in Canada and provides the reader with a comprehensive and up-to-date account of the neglect, hardship and marginalization endured by First Nations in their relationship with the nation of Canada, and how that marginalization is beginning to change for the better.

Dragland, Stan. (1994). *Floating Voice: Duncan Campbell Scott and the Literature of Treaty 9*. Toronto: Anansi.

A fascinating account of Scott's trips in 1905 and 1906 as a Treaty Commissioner taking Treaty 9 to the First Nations bands in northwestern and northeastern Ontario and along the coast of James Bay. Dragland considers Scott's role as bureaucrat for Indian Affairs and as one of Canada's foremost poets, through his letters, poems, stories and journals, as well as those of his fellow commissioners. For Dragland, Scott "epitomizes the misguided efforts of well-meaning men."

Dumont, James. (1993). *Aboriginal Peoples and the Justice System.* Report of the National Round Table on Aboriginal Justice Issues. Toronto: Canada Communication Group.

James Dumont, former professor in Native Studies at the University of Sudbury and well-known Midewiwin medicine person, gives us an insider's perspective on traditional Aboriginal values, beginning with the seven traditional values of the *Anishinaabe* (Ojibwe and Algonquin) people, and comparing these traditional values with other Aboriginal traditions. By so doing he offers us a glimpse into the value conflicts which so often arise between aboriginal and non-aboriginal people, particularly in the context of the Canadian justice system.

Edwards, Peter. (2001). *One Dead Indian.* Toronto: Stoddart Publishing.

In this riveting book that tells the story behind the death of Dudley George at Ipperwash in 1995, Edwards, an investigative reporter for the *Toronto Star*, examines the role of then-Premier Mike Harris and the OPP by uncovering sources that reveal the extent of their involvement in this deadly fiasco. *One Dead Indian* makes the reader think outside the box in the exploration of the relations between Canadians and First Nations.

Foster, Michael K. (1982). "Canada's First Languages."
Language and Society, No. 7, pp. 7-16.

Michael Foster provides us with some important insights into the multiplicity of languages in Canada alone. In Canada there are 11 separate indigenous language families. Each language family is as distinct from the others as a European language family would be from Chinese or Japanese. Within each of these families there are a number of languages, which though they bear a relationship to one another and probably come from a common source, are distinct enough from one another to be regarded as distinct languages in themselves—so that there are in total 53 distinct indigenous languages spoken in Canada.

Frideres, James S. (1993). *Native Peoples in Canada: Contemporary Conflicts*. (4th Edition). Scarborough: Prentice Hall.

Frideres provides us with an overview of the history of relations between First Nations and the nation of Canada, with a clarification of the term *Native,* and with the various political and legal distinctions that have emerged in Canada. The complex and often divisive distinctions between status and non-status Indian, treaty and non-treaty, Inuit and Métis are presented as political and legal conveniences which tend to overlook the great heterogeneity of Aboriginal peoples and cloud the contemporary pan-Indian movement.

Miller, David R, Carl Beal, James Dempsey and R. Wesley
Heber (eds.). (1992). *The First Ones: Readings in Indian/
Native Studies.* Saskatoon: Saskatchewan Indian Federated
College Press.

This collection of readings discusses the development
of Indian/Native studies in Canada and expands on the changes
which have occurred in the philosophies and directions of
various Native Studies programs at the post-secondary level.
Most departments of Native Studies take an interdisciplinary
approach to the "study" of First Nations peoples and issues
with an interest in providing students, both Native and non-
Native alike, with a range of alternatives for critical thinking
and perceiving in relation to the human/global condition.

Richardson, Boyce. (1993). *People of Terra Nullius.* Toronto:
Douglas and McIntyre.

Boyce Richardson writes on the Anishnaabe who are
referred to as *Algonquin.* The Algonquins were among the first
Native people that the Europeans came into contact with. They
once held sway over a vast tract of land that included the Ottawa
River and the present city of Ottawa. Richardson gives us a bit
of the history of the Algonquin since contact and the effects
that colonization had on them, and continues to have on
contemporary Algonquins who are still trying to preserve their
traditional way of life.

Richardson, Boyce (ed.). (1989). *Drumbeat: Anger and Renewal in Indian Country.* Toronto: Summerhill Press and Assembly of First Nations, pp. 265-294.

Certainly few would disagree with the authors in this anthology that, "In nearly two hundred years of contact, Aboriginal people have learned far more about the white man than white men have learned of the First Peoples in North America" (p. 292). The optimistic news is that many non-Aboriginal people are beginning to educate themselves about Aboriginal realities, experiences and traditions.

Titley, Brian. (1986). *A Narrow Vision: Duncan Campbell Scott and the Administration of Indian Affairs in Canada.* Vancouver: University of British Columbia Press.

Titley examines Scott's role as a civil servant and policy arbiter in the Department of Indian Affairs "in a particularly turbulent and eventful era."

Widdowson, Frances and Albert Howard. (2008). *Disrobing the Aboriginal Industry: The Deception Behind Indigenous Cultural Preservation.* Kingston and Montreal: McGill-Queen's University Press.

Widdowson and Howard argue that continued Native marginalization in Canada despite billions of dollars expended by government is the result of an "Aboriginal Industry" made up largely of non-Aboriginal lawyers, consultants and bureaucrats who promote well-intended but wrong-headed policies such as land claims and self government.

Notes on the Author and Illustrators

Roger Spielmann, PhD, is from Sudbury, Ontario, Canada, where he has been a member of the Native Studies department at the University of Sudbury (federated with Laurentian University) since 1990. He is currently an Associate Professor. Though he is non-Native, he lived for 11 years in the Algonquin community of Pikogan (1979-1990) where he was involved in a number of research, teaching and curriculum projects and was fortunate to become conversationally fluent in the Algonquin language. From 1983-1990 he served as the Coordinator of the Algonquin Language and Culture Program at Amo Ososwan School in the community of Winneway. The University of Toronto Press published his book, *"You're So Fat!": Exploring Ojibwe Discourse* in 1998, and reprinted it in 2003.

Perry McLeod-Shabogesic of the "Crane Clan" is an Ojibway Anishnaabe from N'biising (Nipissing) First Nation (NFN) located on the north shores of Lake Nipissing in Northern Ontario, Canada. Perry has been an artist, cartoonist, writer, traditional helper, medicine harvester and cultural resource person in and around his community for many years. Perry's spirit name is "Aandzooked," which means "Teller of sacred stories" in Ojibway.

Perry's comic strip *Baloney & Bannock* has slowly become a cult favourite among many Anishinabek communities. He worked closely with world renowned cartoonist Lynn Johnston (*For Better or For Worse*), helping her develop story lines for her strip as well as improving his own techniques.

From politics to culture, he loves to poke fun. His sense of humour has even caused him to get into a little controversy along the way. On this matter Perry says "If you can't laugh at yourself and the world around you, then I'm more than willing to help ya!"

Tim Steven is an illustrator and fine artist living near Toronto, Ontario, Canada. His work has been recognized at local, national and international levels, and hangs in many private and corporate collections, including the permanent collection of The University of Western Ontario. In the period from the mid 1980s to mid 1990s Tim owned a mid size graphic design studio in London, Ontario. From the mid 1990s to 2002 he worked from his home/studio as well as teaching drawing and illustration courses part-time at Fanshawe College in London. Since then he has moved freely between commercial assignments and painting.